THE ENCYCLOPEDIA OF PSYCHOACTIVE DRUGS

SERIES 1

SERIES 2

BRAIN
FUNCTION

THE ENCYCLOPEDIA OF PSYCHOACTIVE DRUGS
SERIES 2
BRAIN FUNCTION

PAUL NORDSTROM AUGUST

CHELSEA HOUSE PUBLISHERS
NEW YORK • NEW HAVEN • PHILADELPHIA

EDITOR-IN-CHIEF: Nancy Toff
EXECUTIVE EDITOR: Remmel T. Nunn
MANAGING EDITOR: Karyn Gullen Browne
COPY CHIEF: Juliann Barbato
PICTURE EDITOR: Adrian G. Allen
ART DIRECTOR: Giannella Garrett
MANUFACTURING MANAGER: Gerald Levine

Staff for BRAIN FUNCTION:

SENIOR EDITOR: Jane Larkin Crain
ASSOCIATE EDITOR: Paula Edelson
ASSISTANT EDITOR: Laura-Ann Dolce
COPY EDITOR: Ellen Scordato
ASSOCIATE PICTURE EDITOR: Juliette Dickstein
PICTURE RESEARCHER: Villette Harris
DESIGNER: Victoria Tomaselli
ASSISTANT DESIGNER: Donna Sinisgalli
PRODUCTION COORDINATOR: Joseph Romano
COVER ILLUSTRATION: The Bettmann Archive

CREATIVE DIRECTOR: Harold Steinberg

3 5 7 9 8 6 4 2
Library of Congress Cataloging in Publication Data

August, Paul.
  Brain function.
  (The Encyclopedia of psychoactive drugs. Series 2)
  Bibliography: p.
  1. Brain—Juvenile literature. 2. Brain—Effect of drugs on—Juvenile literature.
3. Psychotropic drugs—Juvenile literature. [1. Brain. 2. Brain—Effect of drugs on.
3. Psychotropic drugs. 4. Drugs]
I. Title. II. Series.
QP376.A94 1987   612'.82   87-7989

ISBN 1-55546-204-9

CONTENTS

Brain function is essential to all human survival, emotion, behavior, and activity. Even simple acts, such as browsing at a book fair, require a fantastically complicated series of neurological actions.

FOREWORD

In the Mainstream
of American Life

One of the legacies of the social upheaval of the 1960s is that psychoactive drugs have become part of the mainstream of American life. Schools, homes, and communities cannot be "drug proofed." There is a demand for drugs — and the supply is plentiful. Social norms have changed and drugs are not only available—they are everywhere.

But where efforts to curtail the supply of drugs and outlaw their use have had tragically limited effects on demand, it may be that education has begun to stem the rising tide of drug abuse among young people and adults alike.

Over the past 25 years, as drugs have become an increasingly routine facet of contemporary life, a great many teenagers have adopted the notion that drug taking was somehow a right or a privilege or a necessity. They have done so, however, without understanding the consequences of drug use during the crucial years of adolescence.

The teenage years are few in the total life cycle, but critical in the maturation process. During these years adolescents face the difficult tasks of discovering their identity, clarifying their sexual roles, asserting their independence, learning to cope with authority, and searching for goals that will give their lives meaning.

Drugs rob adolescents of precious time, stamina, and health. They interrupt critical learning processes, sometimes forever. Teenagers who use drugs are likely to withdraw increasingly into themselves, to "cop out" at just the time when they most need to reach out and experience the world.

Solomon Snyder, M.D. at work in his laboratory. During the 1970s and 1980s Snyder and other neuroscientists have accumulated a remarkable amount of knowledge about the workings of the brain.

Fortunately, as a recent Gallup poll shows, young people are beginning to realize this, too. They themselves label drugs their most important problem. In the last few years, moreover, the climate of tolerance and ignorance surrounding drugs has been changing.

Adolescents as well as adults are becoming aware of mounting evidence that every race, ethnic group, and class is vulnerable to drug dependency.

Recent publicity about the cost and failure of drug rehabilitation efforts; dangerous drug use among pilots, air traffic controllers, star athletes, and Hollywood celebrities; and drug-related accidents, suicides, and violent crime have focused the public's attention on the need to wage an all-out war on drug abuse before it seriously undermines the fabric of society itself.

The anti-drug message is getting stronger and there is evidence that the message is beginning to get through to adults and teenagers alike.

The Encyclopedia of Psychoactive Drugs hopes to play a part in the national campaign now underway to educate young people about drugs. Series 1 provides clear and comprehensive discussions of common psychoactive substances, outlines their psychological and physiological effects on the mind and body, explains how they "hook" the user, and separates fact from myth in the complex issue of drug abuse.

Whereas Series 1 focuses on specific drugs, such as nicotine or cocaine, Series 2 confronts a broad range of both social and physiological phenomena. Each volume addresses the ramifications of drug use and abuse on some aspect of human experience: social, familial, cultural, historical, and physical. Separate volumes explore questions about the effects of drugs on brain chemistry and unborn children; the use and abuse of painkillers; the relationship between drugs and sexual behavior, sports, and the arts; drugs and disease; the role of drugs in history; and the sophisticated drugs now being developed in the laboratory that will profoundly change the future.

Each book in the series is fully illustrated and is tailored to the needs and interests of young readers. The more adolescents know about drugs and their role in society, the less likely they are to misuse them.

Joann Rodgers
Senior Editorial Consultant

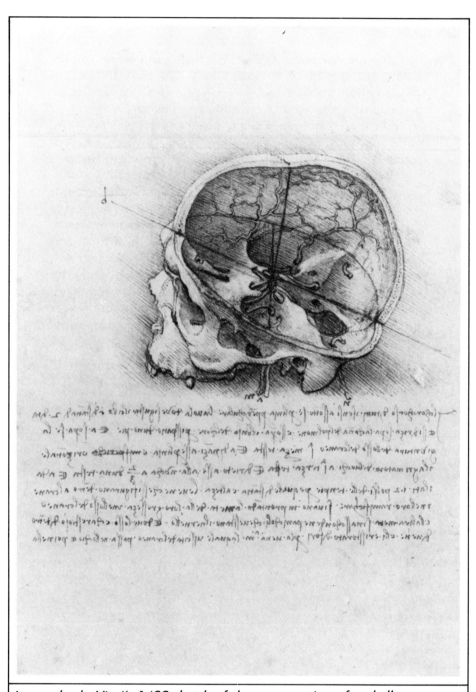

Leonardo da Vinci's 1489 sketch of the cross section of a skull. Leonardo's theories on the brain were considered revolutionary during the Renaissance but have since proven to be inaccurate.

INTRODUCTION

The Gift of Wizardry
Use and Abuse

JACK H. MENDELSON, M.D.
NANCY K. MELLO, Ph.D.
Alcohol and Drug Abuse Research Center
Harvard Medical School—McLean Hospital

Dorothy to the Wizard:

"I think you are a very bad man," said Dorothy.
"Oh no, my dear; I'm really a very good man; but I'm a very bad Wizard."
—from THE WIZARD OF OZ

Man is endowed with the gift of wizardry, a talent for discovery and invention. The discovery and invention of substances that change the way we feel and behave are among man's special accomplishments, and, like so many other products of our wizardry, these substances have the capacity to harm as well as to help. Psychoactive drugs can cause profound changes in the chemistry of the brain and other vital organs, and although their legitimate use can relieve pain and cure disease, their abuse leads in a tragic number of cases to destruction.

Consider alcohol — available to all and yet regarded with intense ambivalence from biblical times to the present day. The use of alcoholic beverages dates back to our earliest ancestors. Alcohol use and misuse became associated with the worship of gods and demons. One of the most powerful Greek gods was Dionysus, lord of fruitfulness and god of wine. The Romans adopted Dionysus but changed his name to Bacchus. Festivals and holidays associated with Bacchus celebrated the harvest and the origins of life. Time has blurred the images of the Bacchanalian festival, but the theme of

13

drunkenness as a major part of celebration has survived the pagan gods and remains a familiar part of modern society. The term "Bacchanalian Festival" conveys a more appealing image than "drunken orgy" or "pot party," but whatever the label, drinking alcohol is a form of drug use that results in addiction for millions.

The fact that many millions of other people can use alcohol in moderation does not mitigate the toll this drug takes on society as a whole. According to reliable estimates, one out of every ten Americans develops a serious alcohol-related problem sometime in his or her lifetime. In addition, automobile accidents caused by drunken drivers claim the lives of tens of thousands every year. Many of the victims are gifted young people, just starting out in adult life. Hospital emergency rooms abound with patients seeking help for alcohol-related injuries.

Who is to blame? Can we blame the many manufacturers who produce such an amazing variety of alcoholic beverages? Should we blame the educators who fail to explain the perils of intoxication, or so exaggerate the dangers of drinking that no one could possibly believe them? Are friends to blame — those peers who urge others to "drink more and faster," or the macho types who stress the importance of being able to "hold your liquor"? Casting blame, however, is hardly constructive, and pointing the finger is a fruitless way to deal with the problem. Alcoholism and drug abuse have few culprits but many victims. Accountability begins with each of us, every time we choose to use or misuse an intoxicating substance.

It is ironic that some of man's earliest medicines, derived from natural plant products, are used today to poison and to intoxicate. Relief from pain and suffering is one of society's many continuing goals. Over 3,000 years ago, the Therapeutic Papyrus of Thebes, one of our earliest written records, gave instructions for the use of opium in the treatment of pain. Opium, in the form of its major derivative, morphine, and similar compounds, such as heroin, have also been used by many to induce changes in mood and feeling. Another example of man's misuse of a natural substance is the coca leaf, which for centuries was used by the Indians of Peru to reduce fatigue and hunger. Its modern derivative, cocaine, has important medical use as a local anesthetic. Unfortunately, its increasing abuse in the 1980s clearly has reached epidemic proportions.

The purpose of this series is to explore in depth the psychological and behavioral effects that psychoactive drugs have on the individual, and also, to investigate the ways in which drug use influences the legal, economic, cultural, and even moral aspects of societies. The information presented here (and in other books in this series) is based on many clinical and laboratory studies and other observations by people from diverse walks of life.

Over the centuries, novelists, poets, and dramatists have provided us with many insights into the sometimes seductive but ultimately problematic aspects of alcohol and drug use. Physicians, lawyers, biologists, psychologists, and social scientists have contributed to a better understanding of the causes and consequences of using these substances. The authors in this series have attempted to gather and condense all the latest information about drug use and abuse. They have also described the sometimes wide gaps in our knowledge and have suggested some new ways to answer many difficult questions.

One such question, for example, is how do alcohol and drug problems get started? And what is the best way to treat them when they do? Not too many years ago, alcoholics and drug abusers were regarded as evil, immoral, or both. It is now recognized that these persons suffer from very complicated diseases involving deep psychological and social problems. To understand how the disease begins and progresses, it is necessary to understand the nature of the substance, the behavior of addicts, and the characteristics of the society or culture in which they live.

Although many of the social environments we live in are very similar, some of the most subtle differences can strongly influence our thinking and behavior. Where we live, go to school and work, whom we discuss things with — all influence our opinions about drug use and misuse. Yet we also share certain commonly accepted beliefs that outweigh any differences in our attitudes. The authors in this series have tried to identify and discuss the central, most crucial issues concerning drug use and misuse.

Despite the increasing sophistication of the chemical substances we create in the laboratory, we have a long way to go in our efforts to make these powerful drugs work for us rather than against us.

The volumes in this series address a wide range of timely questions. What influence has drug use had on the arts? Why do so many of today's celebrities and star athletes use drugs, and what is being done to solve this problem? What is the relationship between drugs and crime? What is the physiological basis for the power drugs can hold over us? These are but a few of the issues explored in this far-ranging series.

Educating people about the dangers of drugs can go a long way towards minimizing the desperate consequences of substance abuse for individuals and society as a whole. Luckily, human beings have the resources to solve even the most serious problems that beset them, once they make the commitment to do so. As one keen and sensitive observer, Dr. Lewis Thomas, has said,

> There is nothing at all absurd about the human condition. We matter. It seems to me a good guess, hazarded by a good many people who have thought about it, that we may be engaged in the formation of something like a mind for the life of this planet. If this is so, we are still at the most primitive stage, still fumbling with language and thinking, but infinitely capacitated for the future. Looked at this way, it is remarkable that we've come as far as we have in so short a period, really no time at all as geologists measure time. We are the newest, youngest, and the brightest thing around.

BRAIN
FUNCTION

Auguste Rodin's sculpture "The Thinker." What differentiates human beings from the rest of the animal kingdom is the human brain's capacity to hold and express profound thoughts.

AUTHOR'S PREFACE

An examination of any human situation reveals just a few of the operations performed or controlled by the brain. The author, for instance, sits at a computer (itself the amazing product of human brains), deciphering handwritten material and almost instantaneously typing it into the word processor. This one act is made of many smaller ones: the visualization and translation into language of the written symbols on the original draft; consideration and occasional spontaneous revision of the phrases within the brain; and coordination of the complex finger movements required to type the sentences at a rate of perhaps 70 or 80 words per minute. Similarly, the reader of this or any text must coordinate precise eye movements and focusing while going down the page; at the same time, the symbols on the page are translated into letters, words, sentences, and meaning. Simultaneously, and perhaps unconsciously, author or reader may be listening to music, drinking a beverage or eating a snack, or daydreaming about other matters entirely!

Another everyday situation demands perhaps even greater coordination of activity and various functions from the brain: the seemingly simple act of driving an automobile. Experienced drivers can operate several dashboard controls at once, converse with other passengers, and use the "special senses" to watch for traffic and street signs, hear sirens or

Alcohol alters the chemistry of the brain, impairing the judgment, reaction time, and coordination that are essential to safe driving.

horns, smell a gas leak, and sense the direction and acceleration of the car. While all this is going on, the driver must coordinate (often "without thinking") the precise movements of hands and feet needed to drive the car carefully and in the desired direction.

These highly simplified descriptions of typical brain activity actually represent only the tip of a neural iceberg. Along with these actions, which are largely voluntary and conscious, the brain is continually monitoring the body's well-being: checking and possibly modifying heart rate, breathing, and blood pressure; maintaining proper body temperature; and constantly keeping in touch with the environment through messages received by the body's sophisticated sensing devices of touch, vision, hearing, taste, and smell. All this, and much more, is carried out automatically and unconsciously by the brain.

The wondrous complexity of the human brain can also be appreciated in an entirely different way — by its capacity to accumulate, communicate, and store knowledge. Human brains manipulate information ranging from ideas about the large-scale structure of the universe to detailed mathematical descriptions of the subatomic "zoo" of quarks, leptons, and other particles that make up atoms, molecules, and the brain itself. In addition, at any given time one's brain is full of the emotions, memories, and sense of purpose that make up one's personality and individual identity — the unique, inexplicable realm of the self and of consciousness. This mysterious private universe — so full of memories, desire, plans, and dreams, and yet so fragile and destined to vanish with its owner's death —is perhaps the essence of human existence.

Brain Malfunction

Unfortunately, human brains do not always function ideally. A variety of diseases, injuries, and inherited conditions can reduce or even prevent proper brain functioning, often with severe or fatal effects. Given the complexity of the brain, it is perhaps unsurprising that there is a potential for such malfunction. For example, nerve cells and fibers can be physically damaged or torn, areas of the brain can be deprived of blood (and thus of nutrients and oxygen), and numerous diseases can affect the brain's ability to work properly. The impairment or complete loss of memory, control of movement, sensation, and higher functions such as judgment can be the terrible result of damage to the brain. Even one's personality can suffer abrupt change after brain injury or certain types of drug abuse.

Small chemical "messengers" known as *neurotransmitters* play a critical role in brain function. Certain diseases and drugs disrupt the functioning of neurotransmitters, which in turn results in a wide range of malfunctions in brain activity. For example, alcohol has a profound effect on driving performance. Drinking even small amounts of beverages containing alcohol — the world's most widely abused psychoactive agent — can greatly impair judgment, reaction time, and coordination, all essential for safe driving. It has been estimated that perhaps four out of five automobile accidents are alcohol-related.

The Neurosciences

In recent years, knowledge about the brain and how it functions (and malfunctions) has been accumulated at a rate faster than that in any previous era. (As with much of biological science, recent technological advances such as "genetic engineering" and computerized imaging processes have contributed greatly to this revolution in neuroscientific research.) As can be imagined when dealing with something so complex, study of the human brain can be approached in many important ways, each one vital to our understanding of what the brain actually does and how it works.

There are several important branches of neuroscience. Molecular neurobiology investigates genes, proteins, and other microscopic elements of neurons and the other cells making up the brain and nervous system. Psychopharmacology focuses not only on the natural neurotransmitters, which act as the chemical "messengers" between neurons, but also on the immense number of psychoactive agents that can affect human mood and behavior. Psychology is the field that investigates such complex brain activities as emotion, memory, dreams, consciousness, and behavior. Psychiatry and neurology are medical specialties dealing with brain disorders. Psychiatrists attempt to diagnose and treat (often with psychoactive drugs) patients suffering from mood or behavioral disorders such as depression, anxiety, or schizophrenia. Neurologists, on the other hand, treat patients with more *organic* brain damage, such as that resulting from disease or injury to the nerves.

Neuroanatomy is one of the oldest of the neurosciences, as early drawings portraying the brain and other elements of the human nervous system attest. Here the emphasis is on the physical structure of the brain, from the microscopic level of the neuron and the brain's other supporting cells to macroscopic (visible with the naked eye) functional regions and the connections between them.

Of course, the brain is studied in many ways, and it should be noted that this list is not conclusive. Moreover, much research in each branch of the neurosciences overlaps that in others. Current research on the mental illness schizophrenia, for instance, links the psychiatric evaluation of psychological and behavioral changes exhibited by persons with this illness to molecular studies of abnormal levels of receptors for the neurotransmitter dopamine. (See Chapter 8.)

This book draws on the results of neuroscientific research and describes the specific regions of the brain, each of which is involved in a particular aspect of brain function. Chapter 1 takes the reader on a brief tour of the various parts of the human nervous system. Chapter 2 describes the general structure of the brain and spinal cord in greater detail and locates the specific regions discussed in subsequent chapters. Chapters 3 through 7 take a closer look at specific brain regions and functions, such as control of breathing and consciousness; control of movement; general sensation; the special senses; behavior, emotions, and memory; and langauge comprehension and production.

Chapter 8 briefly describes several common conditions in which the brain functions improperly and discusses possible links between psychoactive drugs and some of these disorders.

This volume represents something of a departure from other books in *The Encyclopedia of Psychoactive Drugs*, most of which are concerned with one or more specific psychoactive agents. It is hoped, however, that this general introduction to the brain and how it functions will not only interest readers but also assist them in better understanding how psychoactive drugs can affect mood, behavior, and other brain and bodily functions.

Certainly, some aspects of brain function — its neuroanatomical basis in particular — are notoriously difficult to learn. Young readers may initially find this subject rather daunting. However, study of this subject might be likened to scaling a steep mountain: The climb is long and hard, but the view from the peak is breathtaking.

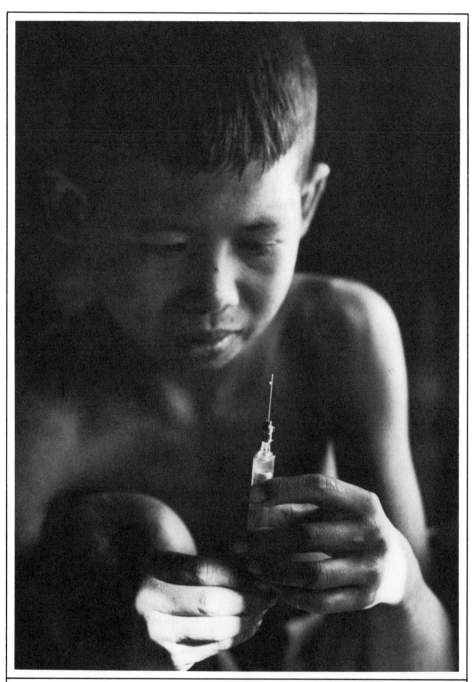

A young heroin addict. Taking any drug, from nicotine to heroin, can disrupt the functioning of the complex network of nerve cells and fibers that makes up the central nervous system.

CHAPTER 1

THE HUMAN NERVOUS SYSTEM

Although the brain itself is central to the various operations described in the Preface, it must first be considered as only one part of a complex network of nerve cells and fibers known as the human nervous system. This may be broken down conveniently into three main divisions: the *central nervous system* (CNS), which includes the brain and the spinal cord; the *peripheral nervous system* (PNS), which comprises the entire nervous system outside the brain and spinal cord; and the *autonomic nervous system* (ANS), which is that portion of the peripheral nervous system that regulates the largely involuntary functions of internal muscles and glands. The ANS is further divided into the sympathetic division and the parasympathetic division. Although some brain functions are performed entirely within the CNS, many others are intimately linked with elements of the peripheral or autonomic nervous systems. This chapter gives an overview of the human nervous system, these three divisions, and how they are organized within the human body.

The Neuron

Neurons are the fundamental components of the human nervous system. There are roughly 10 billion neurons in the human brain, and they come in all sizes and shapes, but all share certain basic features. (See Fig. 1.) The typical neuron

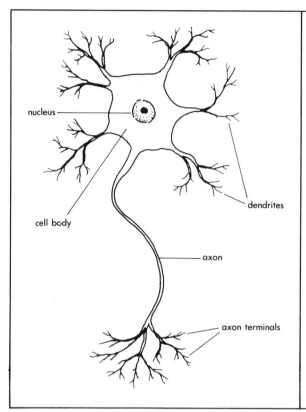

nucleus

cell body

dendrites

axon

axon terminals

Figure 1: An Idealized Neuron. *Axons and dendrites serve as essential links that allow neurons to communicate with each other. Messages are received through the dendrites and transmitted along the axon.*

consists of a cell body, a primary extension known as the axon, and numerous other branches called dendrites. Although neurons have only one axon, they show great variety in the number and complexity of their dendrites. The axon may also be extensively branched. (See Fig. 2.)

The neuron is a cell specialized for the transmission of information, and the axon and dendrites serve as essential links that allow neurons to communicate with one another. Information is carried between neurons by means of neurotransmitters and takes place at junctions between neurons known as *synapses*. (See Fig. 3.) At a synapse, the axon of one neuron nearly makes contact with the dendrite (or, in some cases, the cell body or axon) of another neuron. The end of the axon, when properly stimulated, releases neurotransmitters contained in tiny saclike *vesicles* into the region between the two neurons. These molecules then reach specific receptors located on the second neuron, which then becomes stimulated in its own right. The way in which the second neuron is affected depends greatly on which of the many known neurotransmitters is involved. A neurotransmitter can stimulate a neuron to release neurotransmitters of its own, or prevent it from firing. Many psychoactive drugs have their effects by mimicking, enhancing, preventing, or

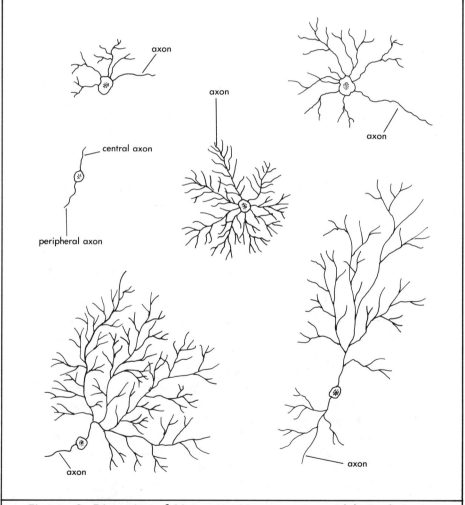

Figure 2: Diversity of Neurons. *Neurons vary widely in their size, shape, and the number and complexity of their dendrites.*

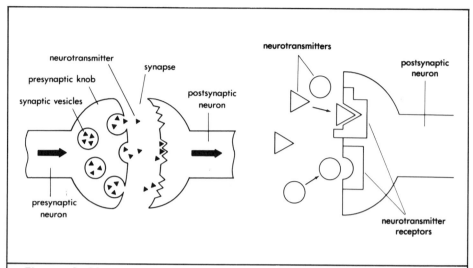

Figure 3: Neurotransmitter Activity. The drawing on the left shows how one neuron signals another across the synapse by emitting neurotransmitters. The drawing on the right shows how each kind of neurotransmitter fits only one kind of receptor on the target neuron.

otherwise modifying the normal actions of neurotransmitters on receptors. Cocaine, for example, produces its effects by enhancing the activity of the neurotransmitters dopamine and norepinephrine, whereas opiates such as heroin mimic neurotransmitters called endorphins.

Once a neuron is stimulated by a neurotransmitter, information flows within it electrically, in tiny, wavelike pulses. In other words, information has been transformed from a chemical form into an electrical one. These pulses travel down the dendrites of a neuron and into the cell body, where they can meet and combine with pulses arriving from other dendrites. If the total resulting electric stimulation is powerful enough, the neuron's axon becomes stimulated, and goes on to release its own neurotransmitters at synapses and thus to transmit information to still other neurons.

Although this simple description of neuronal activity uses the word "information," and although much is known about neurotransmitters and the electrical behavior of neurons, how such chemical and electrical stimulation of nerves results in the transmission of ideas, memories, or other "messages" is still a great mystery.

The Central Nervous System

The central nervous system (CNS) consists of the brain and the spinal cord, which is a continuation of the lower part of the brain itself. The critical importance of the CNS for human life is illustrated by its protective encasement in bone: The brain is securely enclosed in the skull and the spinal cord is surrounded by the strong *vertebrae* of the backbone. Damage to these protective structures — for instance, a broken neck or a badly fractured skull—can result in immediate death.

The organization and contents of the central nervous system are considered in the following chapter.

The Peripheral Nervous System

The peripheral nervous system can be classified into two main groups of nerves. *Spinal nerves* arise from the spinal cord and are systematically distributed throughout the body from the neck down. The 12 *cranial nerves* have their origins in the brain itself. These important nerves not only act as spinal nerves for the head and neck, but also are involved in the "special senses" and important autonomic functions, as described below.

Spinal Nerves

As with most features of the human nervous system, the spinal nerves are paired — that is, there is one each for the right and left sides of the body. Each pair of spinal nerves leaves the spinal cord through gaps between adjacent vertebrae, which are the bones that make up the spine.

Spinal nerves are organized into bundles, each of which contains two main types of nerve fibers, *sensory* and *motor*. These carry information in opposite directions, just as one might suspect after considering the different roles they play. Sensory nerve fibers carry information from a variety of sensory receptors located in the skin, muscles, and joints; this information must thus travel toward the spinal cord and then up to the brain for further processing. Motor fibers, on the other hand, carry information from the brain, down the spinal cord, and through the spinal nerve to the relevant muscle.

Cranial Nerves

The 12 pairs of important cranial nerves are located in the brain and serve the motor and sensory functions of spinal nerves for the head and neck, as well as handling certain special functions of their own. Each of the cranial nerves participates in one or more of the following operations: carrying motor and sensory information to various regions of the head and neck; serving as the "wiring system" for the "special senses" of vision, hearing and balance, taste, and smell; and transmitting autonomic information to special glands and organs.

A few examples of cranial nerves may help to explain the types of roles they play. The *trigeminal nerve* is a "mixed" nerve that carries sensations to the brain as well as controlling several important muscles (the strong jaw muscles for chewing). The *facial nerve* sends branches to the important facial muscles of expression — those used in smiling, frowning, raising one's eyebrows, and so forth. (This nerve thus plays an obviously critical role in the expression of emotions.) The *olfactory* and *optic nerves* are "special sense" nerves, and carry visual and olfactory (smell) input from the eyes and nose to the brain for processing. The *oculomotor nerve* controls eye movements and is also involved in focusing images on the retina. The crucial *vagus nerve*, along with performing sensory and motor functions, sends autonomic nerve fibers to the heart, stomach, and intestines to help regulate their activity.

The Autonomic Nervous System

The functions of the autonomic nervous system (ANS) are partly suggested by other names previously used to describe it: the "vegetative" or "involuntary" nervous system. Although the ANS has definite links with both the peripheral and central nervous systems, it remains largely outside conscious, voluntary control. Its two subdivisions, the sympathetic division and the parasympathetic division, both play important roles in the day-to-day functioning of the human body. In general, the parasympathetic division controls the routine "vegetative" functions such as digestion. The sympathetic division functions as the arousal center during emergencies or stress situations.

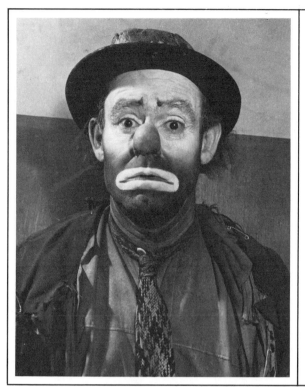

Emmet Kelly, the world's most famous clown. Kelly's marvelous powers of expression are governed by the facial nerve, 1 of 12 cranial nerves located in the brain.

As can be seen in Figure 4, the sympathetic and para-sympathetic divisions of the ANS often supply the same organ, but they generally have very different or even opposing effects. For example, sympathetic stimulation of the heart leads to an increase in heart rate, whereas parasympathetic nerves cause the heart to slow down. In this way, the sympathetic division of the ANS is like an "accelerator" for the heart, and the parasympathetic division is like a "brake"; heart rate at any one moment reflects the degree of activity of each set of nerves. Similarly, sympathetic nerves are responsible for dilation of the eye's pupil, whereas parasympathetic nerves cause the pupil to contract.

The Sympathetic Division

As we have said, the sympathetic division of the ANS functions in stressful "fight or flight" situations — such as when one is chased by a vicious dog, goes on a first date, or takes a difficult exam. Sympathetic nerves help the body to respond to such stress, in part by acting on the following organs and systems:

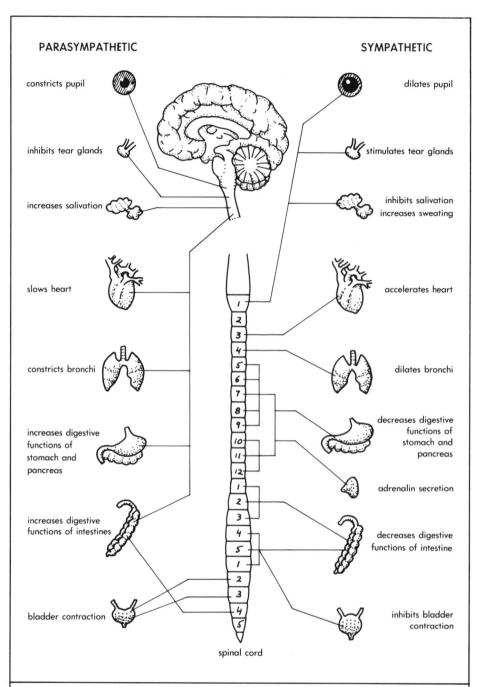

Figure 4: The Autonomic Nervous System. *The parasympathetic and sympathetic divisions of the ANS often send nerve signals to the same organ, but they generally have opposing effects.*

•The adrenal medulla: In stressful situations, sympathetic nerves cause the adrenal medulla, an important gland located above the kidney, to release the neurotransmitter epinephrine, also known as adrenaline. This action serves to increase the heart rate, increase blood pressure (by causing the contraction of small muscles in blood vessels), and divert blood flow from the skin (causing a pale appearance) and gastrointestinal region to limb muscles important for self-defense. The release of epinephrine also causes an increase in the amount of glucose in the blood. This sugar molecule, released from storage in the liver, is used for energy by muscles as part of the "fight or flight" reaction.

•The eye: As mentioned earlier, sympathetic nerves dilate the pupils of the eyes when the body is under stress. This is due to the effect of sympathetic nerves on muscles within the eye.

•The skin: In addition to paleness caused by decreased blood flow to the skin, sweat glands are activated — leading to sweating of the palms and brow — and muscles that cause hair to stand on end are stimulated, leading to "gooseflesh" in humans and more dramatic displays of "hair-raising" in cats and other mammals.

•The respiratory system: As can be expected, the response to a stressful situation calls for plenty of oxygen (which is used, along with glucose, to produce energy). Sympathetic nerves cause muscles along the airways to relax, thus allowing more air to flow into the lungs and more oxygen to enter the bloodstream.

Apart from such natural sympathetic activities, the sympathetic division of the ANS may be affected by several psychoactive drugs. Primarily by mimicking or prolonging the actions of epinephrine and the similar neurotransmitter norepinephrine, cocaine and amphetamines can have dangerous side effects such as increasing the heart rate or causing an irregular cardiac rhythm, raising the blood pressure, and possibly causing a stroke. (See Chapter 8.)

The Parasympathetic Division

The effects of parasympathetic nerves are dramatically different from those of sympathetic nerves, being much more involved with so-called "vegetative" bodily functions such as

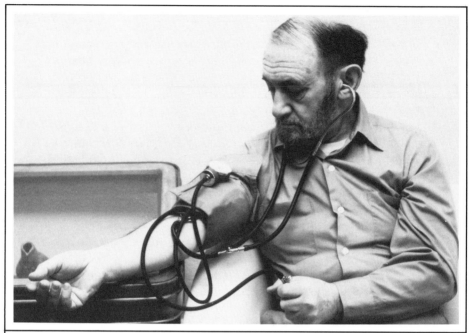

One of the several effects the parasympathetic nerves have on the cardiovascular system is to reduce blood pressure.

the digestion of food and excretion of waste than with the stress situations handled by the sympathetic division. There are a number of important parasympathetic functions:

•The cardiovascular system: Parasympathetic effects on the cardiovascular system are almost the opposite of sympathetic effects. Parasympathetic nerves decrease the heart rate and reduce blood pressure. These nerves also maximize blood flow to the stomach, liver, intestines, and other organs involved in digestion.

•The gastrointestinal system: In addition to this increased blood flow to the stomach, liver, and intestines, parasympathetic nerves activate other mechanisms of eating and digestion. These include increased salivation, the release into the stomach and intestine of the important chemical "juices" needed for digesting food, and stimulation of muscles in the intestinal wall to promote the movement of food through the digestive system.

•The eye: Parasympathetic nerve fibers cause contraction of the pupil and allow the focusing of the eye on close objects, an activity known as *accommodation*. (Ophthalmologists — eye doctors — use drugs that cancel these parasympathetic effects, thus causing the pupil to dilate and allowing the eye to be more readily examined. These drugs also disrupt accommodation, so that the patient typically cannot read for several hours thereafter.)

These are but a few of the many parasympathetic actions. As with the sympathetic division of the ANS, drugs can influence parasympathetic functions. Marijuana, for instance, has an antiparasympathetic action, leading to dilated pupils, a "dry mouth" from decreased salivation, and an increased heart rate caused by the loss of parasympathetic "braking" activity on the heart.

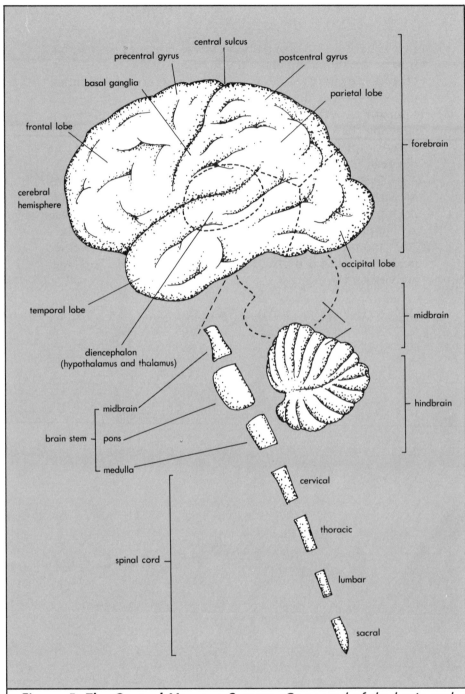

Figure 5: The Central Nervous System. Composed of the brain and the spinal cord, the CNS governs mental activities and voluntary acts.

CHAPTER 2

A BRIEF TOUR OF THE CENTRAL NERVOUS SYSTEM

The central nervous system (CNS) is certainly the most vital part of the human nervous system. It is composed of the brain and spinal cord and governs consciousness, mental activities, and voluntary acts, among other neural activities. (See Fig. 5.) A familiarity with its basic organization is essential to an understanding of the detailed workings of the brain.

The Spinal Cord

The spinal cord is a column of neural tissue that runs downward from the brain through the bones of the spinal column. It consists of "gray matter" surrounded by "white matter." (See Fig. 6.) The gray matter, which is shaped rather like a butterfly, is made up of the bodies of neurons and other cells. In general the front "wings" of the gray matter contain the motor neurons, which are involved in muscular activity and movement. The posterior region is concerned with sensory activity.

The white matter consists of bundles of long nerve fibers that link specific brain regions to other parts of the body. These tracts of fibers run in both directions — some (referred to as "ascending") carry nerve impulses to the brain, whereas others ("descending") transmit impulses from it. For in-

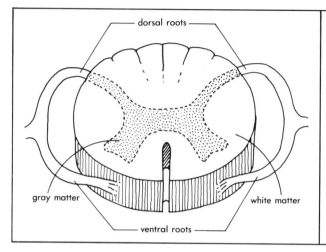

gray matter

white matter

dorsal roots

ventral roots

Figure 6: White Matter and Gray Matter. *The spinal cord consists of white matter (bundles of long nerve fibers) and gray matter (neurons and other cells).*

stance, one group of descending fibers transmits information from the *motor cortex* (in the brain) to *motor neurons* (neurons that stimulate muscle cells) within the spinal cord. These motor neurons then send impulses to groups of muscles throughout the body. Sensory information, on the other hand, travels in the opposite direction; ascending fibers carry sensory impulses from sensory receptors in the skin and organs up through the spinal cord and into the brain.

The Brain

Neuroanatomists have devised several classification schemes to describe the many parts of the brain. One simple scheme divides the brain into three general regions: the *brainstem*, the *cerebellum*, and the *forebrain*.

The Brainstem

One of the most important parts of the brain is the brainstem, which is positioned just above the spinal cord. In fact, the brainstem is in one sense a continuation of the spinal cord, for the many ascending and descending tracts traveling between the brain and the spinal cord pass through it as well. Disease in or damage to the brainstem (such as occurs with a broken neck) can lead to permanent injury or death.

Several important clusters of neurons are contained in the brainstem. Ten of the 12 cranial nerves (see Chapter 1) originate in this section of the brain. These neurons coordinate visual activities such as reading, and also reflex movements such as turning the head toward a sudden sound, or contraction of the pupil of the eye in response to a bright light stimulus.

Another important cluster of neurons in the brainstem is the reticular formation (RF). (See Fig. 7.) These nerve cells are concerned with such bodily functions as breathing, heart activity, and consciousness.

Neurons in the reticular formation exert a great deal of control over the cardiovascular system, most significantly in response to changes in blood pressure. Special pressure receptors in the aorta (the main artery leaving the heart) and

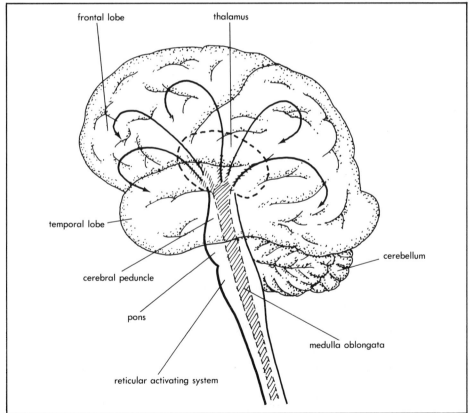

Figure 7: The Reticular Formation. Located in the brain stem, the neurons in the RF play a key role in respiratory and heart activity.

in the carotid artery (which supplies blood to the brain itself) monitor blood pressure. Information from these sensors is used by the cardiovascular center in the reticular formation to raise or lower the heart rate as necessary through sympathetic or parasympathetic fibers.

The reticular formation is of great interest with respect to psychoactive agents, for it is here that many drugs exert their effects. For example, one area of the reticular formation, called the *locus coeruleus* (blue area), controls alertness through the release of the neurotransmitter norepinephrine. (Other neurons in the reticular formation induce sleep by releasing the neurotransmitter serotonin.) Stimulants such as amphetamines and cocaine increase the user's sense of alertness by increasing the concentration of norepinephrine at these synapses. In contrast, depressants such as opiates (heroin and morphine), barbiturates, and other tranquilizers can disrupt the respiration rate — which is maintained by still other reticular nerve cells — by acting on certain receptors in the reticular formation.

The Cerebellum

The cerebellum (Latin for "little brain") is attached to the rear of the brainstem. It is a highly ordered structure concerned primarily with the maintenance of posture and the coordination of muscular activity. (See Chapter 5.)

The Forebrain

The forebrain includes a variety of structures, among them the *hypothalamus*, the *basal ganglia*, and the two large *cerebral hemispheres*.

The hypothalamus is a tiny region lying at the very base of the forebrain. Despite its small size it is immensely important. Through its connections with the *pituitary gland*, the hypothalamus controls the body's *endocrine* (hormone) *system* (a hormone is a chemical product released by endocrine cells into the bloodstream to affect other cells.) In conjunction with the nearby *limbic system*, which is concerned with higher functions such as emotions, the hypothalamus also plays a crucial role in regulating behavior. These topics are further explored in Chapter 6.

The basal ganglia are made up of several clusters of gray matter, all involved in the fine control of movement. Certain substances, such as the compound methylphenyltetrahydropyridine (MPTP), are known to affect these neurons, producing muscular rigidity, difficulties in initiating movement, and tremor — the characteristic symptoms of *Parkinson's disease.* (See Chapter 5.)

The right and left cerebral hemispheres are the most highly evolved portions of the human brain. Their great complexity contrasts dramatically with the brains of other species, in which the cerebral hemispheres are still in primitive stages of evolution. (See Fig. 8.) Among the many important operations carried out by the cerebral hemispheres are the processing of sensory information, the production of language, and the planning of movement. So-called "higher functions," such as prediction, calculation, and judgment are also based in the cerebral hemispheres. It is from this still-mysterious part of the brain that we humans have acquired the unique ability to control ourselves through reason and logic, and — as a result of this ability—to shape the world around us.

Like the rest of the CNS, the cerebral hemispheres contain both gray matter and white matter. Much of the gray matter is located around the outside of each hemisphere, forming a layer known as the *cerebral cortex.* The cortex is divided into various regions, such as the motor cortex, sensory cortex, and visual cortex.

The white matter of the cerebral hemispheres connects various regions of the cerebral cortex with other parts of the CNS. For instance, the motor cortex is linked by descending tracts of fibers to motor neurons in the spinal cord. The majority of white matter, however, links one area of the cerebral cortex with another. One of the most important of these connections, the corpus callosum, links the right and left hemispheres.

Interestingly, the right and left cerebral hemispheres are far from identical, and each carries out different tasks. Such "hemispheric asymmetries," the subject of much current speculation and debate, are considered further in Chapter 7. Perhaps even more surprisingly, one can survive with only one hemisphere: In certain cases of severe neurological disease, an operation known as *hemispherectomy* is done, in

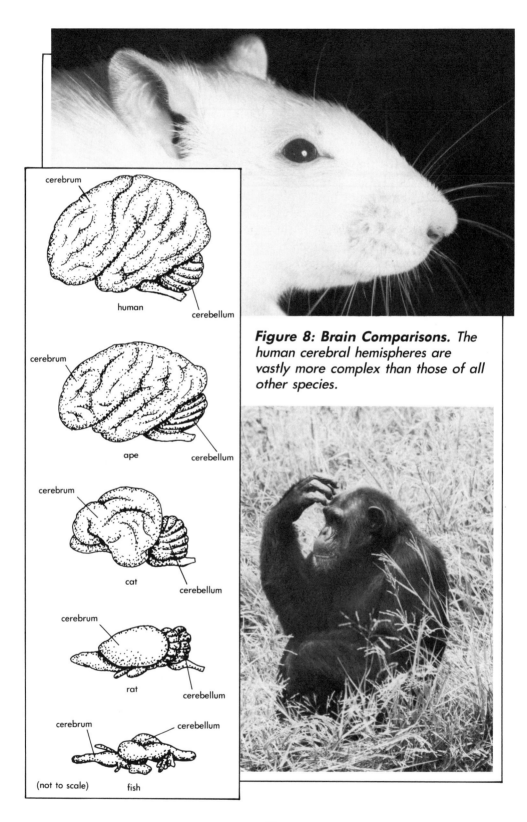

cerebrum

human

cerebellum

cerebrum

ape

cerebellum

cerebrum

cat

cerebellum

cerebrum

rat

cerebellum

cerebrum   cerebellum

(not to scale)   fish

Figure 8: Brain Comparisons. *The human cerebral hemispheres are vastly more complex than those of all other species.*

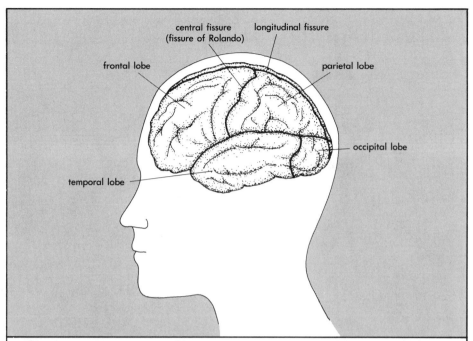

Figure 9: The Lobes of the Brain. *The brain is divided longitudinally into two hemispheres, each of which has four lobes.*

which surgeons remove one hemisphere altogether. Although some functions are undeniably lost, patients who have had this operation can recover to lead healthy lives.

Each of the two hemispheres is divided into four *lobes*. (See Fig.9.) The *frontal lobe* lies roughly below the forehead. It contains the *motor cortex*, which controls movement. A fissure known as the *central sulcus* separates the frontal lobe from the *parietal lobe* behind it. This lobe contains the *sensory cortex*, which helps to analyze sensory information entering the brain from all parts of the body. The *occipital lobe*, in the back of each hemisphere, contains the *visual cortex*, which processes visual information. The visual cortex is linked to the retina of each eye by the optic nerve. The *auditory cortex*, critical to hearing, is situated in the *temporal lobe*. Wernicke's area, which is concerned with comprehension of language, is also situated in the temporal lobe.

The central nervous system is crucial to almost every human function. Without the brain and spinal cord we would not be able to walk, see, hear, feel, or speak. The specific roles this complex system of nerves plays in regard to distinct human functions is what the rest of this book is about.

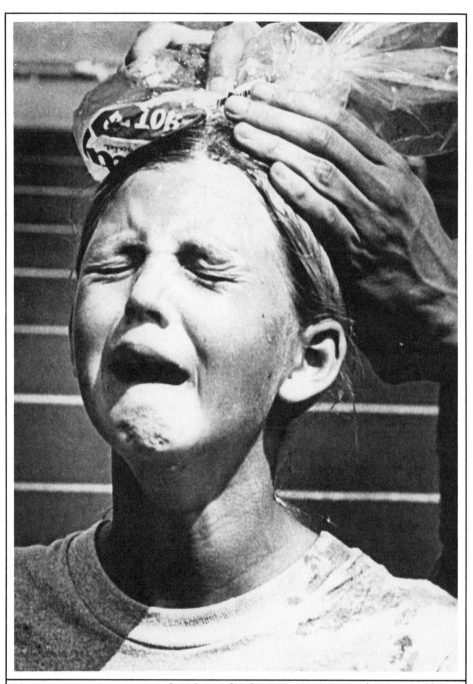

A young runner is treated with ice for heat prostration. She senses the temperature of the ice through a series of neural messages that run from her skin to the brain's sensory cortex.

CHAPTER 3

GENERAL SENSATION

Virtually all human knowledge, emotions, and behavior are based on sensations. One "senses" the activity of one's own body as well as what is occurring in the external environment, and this information, once processed by the central nervous system, generally leads to some sort of reaction. At the most basic level, this response to sensory input can be an automatic reflex, such as the abrupt withdrawal of one's hand from a hot stove or a toe from icy water. (See Chapter 5 for a discussion of these *reflex arcs*.) In more sophisticated ways — some unique to humans — sensations can lead to a variety of more complex responses: rapid and accurate voluntary movements; intense, immediate emotional changes; long-lasting memory storage; and profound intellectual decisions.

Modalities and Receptors

The various sensations perceived all over one's body are classified as various *modalities*: pain, pressure, temperature, vibration, touch, and stretch. Each of these is mediated by sensory *receptors* located in the skin and other organs. Two important types of receptors are *cutaneous receptors*, located in the skin; and *visceral receptors*, which are located in the body's internal organs.

Sensations transmitted from receptors in both the skin and the internal organs travel to the *sensory cortex* of the cerebral hemispheres, where they are consciously recognized and interpreted. This sensory information travels by way of the important *ascending pathways* of the spinal cord and brainstem. There are two main ascending tracts transmitting sensations from the body: one for pain and temperature and one for the other sensory modalities.

The neurons of one ascending tract transmit the crucial sensations of pain and temperature from cutaneous and visceral receptors to the brain. This pathway for pain and temperature messages runs from the receptors through the spinal nerves to the spinal cord; from the spinal cord to the thalamus, the important sensory relay center of the brain; and from the thalamus to the sensory cortex.

Opiate drugs such as morphine and heroin are used widely as *analgesics*, or "painkillers." These substances act on receptors on small neurons in the spinal cord that, when stimulated, inhibit the transmission of painful sensations to the brain. The body's "natural opiates" (small chemical molecules that stimulate opiate receptors throughout the body) can also abolish the sensation of pain in this way, and appear to be involved in acupuncture and other forms of drug-free pain relief.

Sensations of touch, vibration, and position arrive at the spinal cord and then ascend through the rear portion of the spinal cord to the medulla. From the medulla they travel to the thalamus; from there, as with pain and temperature sensations, they are then relayed to the sensory cortex.

The segregation of pain and temperature fibers from those for other sensations has made possible the surgical relief of some forms of severe pain. In the operation known as a *cordotomy*, the spinal pathways for pain are destroyed, thus preventing the transmission of painful sensations.

All sensory modalities for the head and neck are carried by the fifth cranial nerve. As with sensations from the rest of the body, these pass to the sensory cortex by way of a relay in the thalamus.

The Sensory Cortex

The sensory cortex lies in the front of the parietal lobe, just behind the deep fissure called the sulcus that runs across each cerebral hemisphere. (See Fig. 10.) This region of the brain, like the *motor cortex* just in front of it, is organized so that each portion of the sensory cortex receives sensory information from and thus corresponds to one specific part

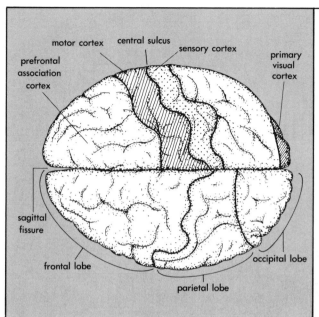

Figure 10: The Sensory Cortex. *This region of the brain helps to analyze sensory information received from all parts of the body.*

of the body. By electrically stimulating each portion of the sensory cortex of volunteers and reporting the sensations they report, researchers were able to "map" the various regions. This map, known as the *sensory homunculus*, is presented in Figure 16 in Chapter 5.

The first thing one notices about this map of the sensory cortex is that not all parts of the body are represented equally or in proportion to their actual size. Rather, the hands, face, and tongue account for a great deal of the sensory cortex, and the trunk and legs for much less. The reasons for this distortion have to do with the fact that not all parts of the body contain the same number of receptors. Much more information is transmitted to the sensory cortex from areas of the body with a high density of receptors, such as the fingertips, than is transmitted from insensitive areas such as the back, which has a relatively low receptor density.

It is both interesting and instructive to compare the sensory cortices of different species. In creatures with highly sensitive whiskers, for instance, a large section of their sensory cortex is devoted to the nose region.

This chapter has explained general sensation — the feelings, such as touch and pain, that are sensed throughout the body. The "special senses" of vision, hearing, balance, smell, and taste are the subject of Chapter 4.

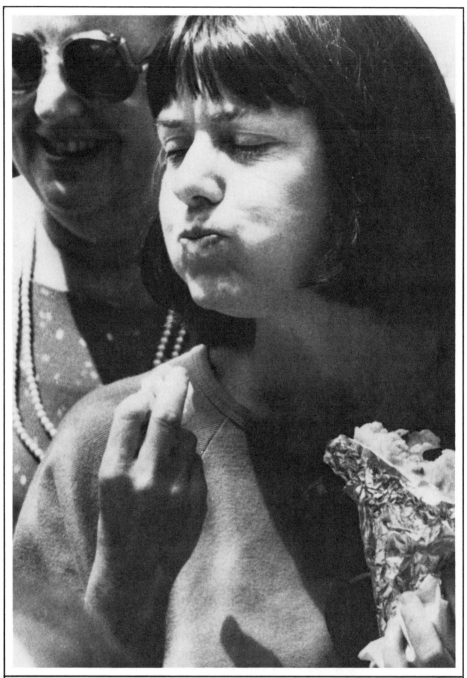

A young girl savors an ethnic delicacy. Taste is detected by taste buds on different parts of the tongue, which can perceive four primary taste sensations: sweet, sour, bitter, and salty.

CHAPTER 4

THE SPECIAL SENSES

Despite the importance of general sensation, most of the sensory information used in daily life is perceived by the special sense organs and analyzed by certain specific brain regions. The fundamentals of the five special senses are presented in this chapter, with special emphasis on the human visual system.

Vision

Humans are highly visual creatures, and large sections of the human brain are devoted to the processing of visual information. Although visual apparatuses have evolved in a number of ways in most species, the human eye is probably the most complex, versatile, and powerful visual instrument on this planet.

The Eye

The eye develops as a direct offshoot of the central nervous system early in gestation — the period of growth of the fetus. Because of this, the optic nerve retains characteristics of the CNS rather than of the peripheral nervous system.

The eye has two main functional parts: the *lens* and the *retina*. The lens serves to focus patterns of light onto the retina, just as a projector lens focuses an image onto a screen.

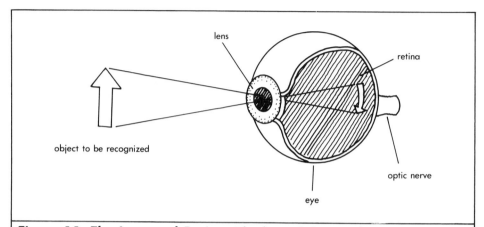

Figure 11: The Lens and Retina. *The lens of the eye focuses patterns of light onto the retina. The image is initially reversed from top to bottom and from right to left.*

As with all simple lens systems, the image is reversed on the retina, as seen in Figure 11; this is compensated for later. The lens's diameter can be modified automatically in a process known as *accommodation*, to allow focusing on near or distant objects. (When this process does not work properly, nearsightedness or farsightedness results.)

The retina is one of nature's true marvels, consisting of a complex arrangement of various types of neurons. The retina may be described as consisting of three layers of cells. The deepest layer is made up of *photoreceptors*, the cells actually responsible for sensing light rays. The neurons of the intermediate layer link the photoreceptors with *ganglion cells*. These are the neurons of the superficial layer and also perform the initial processing of visual information. The long fibers of the ganglion cells join together and leave the back of the retina to form the *optic nerve*. Surprisingly, perhaps, light rays do not hit the photoreceptors directly, but pass through the other two layers first.

Photoreceptors are highly specialized cells and are of two main types, *rods* and *cones*. The cones are responsible for color vision, and each one responds preferentially to red, green, or blue light. (Color blindness is an inherited disorder in which some cones do not develop properly.) In contrast to the cones, the rod cells sense light only in "black and white," but are much more sensitive to low intensities of light than are the cones. Thus, in a dimly lit room or outdoors late at night, objects perceived as being colored in bright light appear only in shades of gray.

Rods and cones are not scattered randomly throughout the retina, but are arranged in quite an orderly way. The center of the retina, the *fovea*, is the region of most acute vision and contains only densely packed cones. Rods are located more peripherally in the retina; this explains why faint objects such as distant stars are best seen when not stared at directly.

Visual Pathways

An image formed on the retina is sensed by the rod and cone cells, and the resulting visual information is sent by the optic nerve to the brain for processing and to participate in several reflexes.

Most of the fibers of the optic nerve carry visual information to the *primary visual cortex* in the rear of the brain for processing. A smaller number of fibers enter the brainstem, where visual reflexes are coordinated.

Analysis of Visual Information

Much of the analysis of visual information takes place in the *visual cortex*, which contains a map of the retina similar to the sensory map described in the previous chapter. Predictably, the region devoted to the fovea (and thus concerned with acute vision) is largest.

Within the visual cortex, different neurons process information about such visual qualities as shape, orientation, and movement. For example, one particular neuron may be stimulated by a straight line oriented vertically, while another, more complex neuron is stimulated by a right angle in motion. *Visual association* areas perform still more sophisticated analysis, including *stereopsis*, or "binocular vision." This permits depth perception, by comparing the slight differences in images presented to the right and left retinas. Another brain region, this one in the temporal lobe, seems to contain complex visual memories. Stimulation of this area causes the subject immediately to visualize complex scenes from the past.

Visual Reflexes

Visual reflexes occur in the brainstem and involve several different functional systems. The *visual turning reflex* links photoreceptors in the peripheral retina (those stimulated by objects on the borders of the visual field) and the muscles of the neck and trunk. This important reflex — a useful protective reaction — causes automatic turning of the head toward a stimulus entering one's field of vision.

The crucial *vestibulo-ocular reflex*, also in the brainstem, permits continued fixation of the eyes on a certain object while the head is turning. In this case, neurons of the retina, the oculomotor system, and the vestibular system (these systems will be discussed later) are concerned. (This sophisticated reflex may be easily demonstrated by readers: First stare at an index finger while turning your head rapidly from side to side, and compare the result with that produced while keeping your head still and waving the finger back and forth.)

The *light reflex*, which is also important, serves to regulate the amount of light entering the eye. When the eye is faced with bright light, muscles cause the pupil to constrict, thus preventing overstimulation of the retina. In dim light the pupil dilates to allow as much light to strike the retina as possible.

Hearing

Just as the visual system translates the visual qualities of light into nerve impulses for analysis by the brain, so does the human auditory system perform a similar operation on sound. Sounds differ most fundamentally in their *frequency*: A canary's song or the sounds made by a flute are of relatively high frequency; deep sounds, such as those of a cello or a foghorn, are of lower frequencies.

Different auditory systems among mammals are specialized to "tune in" to particular sound frequencies. Elephants, for instance, hear low-frequency sounds best, whereas dogs' ears are adjusted to higher frequencies. The bat, which uses its highly sophisticated auditory system much as humans use their visual system, emits and hears sounds of such high frequency that the human ear cannot detect them. Unsurprisingly, human ears work best with sounds within the same range of frequencies as those produced by the human vocal cords—the sounds of normal conversation.

The auditory system is perhaps best understood by following the course of auditory information as it is transformed from environmental sound waves to neuronal impulses within the brain.

The External Ear

Sound waves enter the brain by passing first through the external ear. (For a diagram of the entire ear, see Figure 12.) For humans, this portion of the auditory system is really quite primitive, for it more or less passively receives sounds. Many other animals have special muscles designed to "prick up" and move their ears toward the source of a sound. (The common house cat provides an excellent example of such

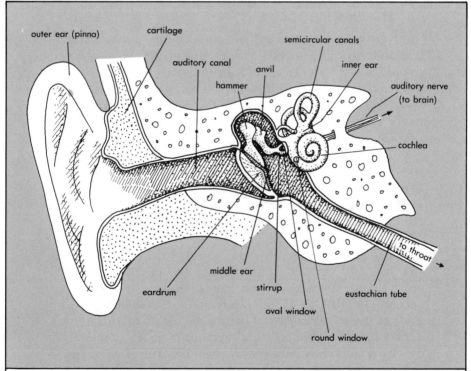

Figure 12: The External, Middle, and Inner Ear. *The sensation of hearing occurs when pressure variations are routed to the cochlea and are translated into patterns of neural activity.*

"directional" ear movement.) The sounds pass, essentially unmodified, through the outer ear canal and hit the *eardrum*. This is a thin membrane stretched across the end of the canal, which vibrates in response to the sound waves striking it.

The Middle Ear

The middle ear contains three important elements of the acoustic system: the hammer, anvil, and stirrup. These delicate bones are attached in such a way as to instantly transmit the vibrations of the eardrum to the fluid-filled *cochlea* of the inner ear. The leverlike arrangement of these *ossicles* (as the hammer, anvil, and stirrup bones are also known) serves to amplify the tiny movements of the eardrum membrane into larger motions more readily appreciated by the receptors of the inner ear.

The Inner Ear

After crossing the external and middle ears, acoustic information is no longer in the form of sound waves but is captured entirely in the movements of the third, stirrup-shaped ossicle. This small bone thus mediates all human perception of sound — from the clap of thunder and the rhythms of rock music to the faint rustle of leaves in the wind and the subtle sound of a cigarette burning.

The base of the stirrup is in contact with the *cochlea* of the inner ear. This is a roughly snail-shaped organ situated in the *spiral labyrinth* of the skull. The key elements of the cochlea are its *hair cells*, a membrane running spirally through it, and the special fluid, known as *endolymph*, that fills it.

The hair cells are covered by tiny, hairlike *cilia* (about one hundred per cell) and are arranged in rows along the spiral of the cochlea. These hair cells are the specialized receptors of the acoustic system and are connected to the ends of the *cochlear nerve* (part of the eighth cranial nerve). Each hair cell is "tuned" to a certain frequency of sound.

As sound waves are transformed into the movements of the three ossicles, the stirrup, by virtue of its contact with a small "window" on the side of the cochlea, causes motion of the cochlear endolymph. This in turn moves a certain portion of the cochlear membrane. The hair cells responding to the specific frequency of each sound wave are stimulated.

Auditory Centers in the Brain

Linked to each hair cell is a cochlear nerve fiber that responds to a specific sound frequency. Bundles of these fibers travel from each ear and pass through the brainstem to the *auditory cortex* in the cerebral hemispheres. As with other sensory cortices, the auditory cortex is "mapped" — the neurons are arranged according to the sound frequency triggering them. Near the auditory cortex in the left hemisphere (in most people) is the important *Wernicke's area*, which is involved in language processing. On the right side of the brain is an area involved in the *emotional* aspects of language. (See Chapter 7.) The appreciation of music is also predominantly a "right-brained" function.

One crucial operation performed on acoustic information involves determining its source, or location of origin. (This is obviously of special importance to predator and prey animals.) This is done in the brainstem, by comparing the differences in sounds reaching each ear.

Also occurring in the brainstem is an important *acoustic reflex* that deals quite simply with arousal. This involves links between the cochlear nerve and the reticular formation — the network of cells in the brainstem that plays an important role in both sleep and arousal. This reticular connection causes alarm clocks (sometimes) to wake us up and loud, unexpected noises of all kinds to startle us. The acoustic reflex has clear protective value.

Balance

Balance might be labeled the "forgotten" special sense, because one is normally unaware of one's maintenance of balance and equilibrium. Nonetheless, this sense, based in the *vestibular system*, is important.

The vestibular system is located in the *vestibular labyrinth*, a complicated structure within the skull, near the spiral labyrinth of the auditory system. There are two functional parts of the vestibular system: the *static* and the *dynamic labyrinths*.

The static labyrinth is concerned with monitoring the position of the head. Special arrangements of *hair cells* (similar to those of the cochlea) are stimulated when the head is tilted from one side to the other or nodded up and down. One reflex associated with this results in the stiffening of leg muscles on the side toward which the head is tilted, to support the extra weight put on that side.

The dynamic labyrinth consists of three semicircular canals, each positioned in a different plane within the skull. The canals are filled with endolymph (a fluid like that in the cochlea), whose motion stimulates groups of hair cells. This system allows the perception of movement and acceleration by monitoring the flow of endolymph through the semicircular canals that results from the rotation of the head in any of three directions (up and down; backwards and forwards; side to side).

Information from the vestibular system is channeled to the brainstem and then to the cerebellum, where it participates in the maintenance of posture and the coordination of movement. The *vestibulo-ocular reflex*, mentioned earlier, depends upon input from the dynamic labyrinth to coordinate fixation of the retina on a desired object while the head is moving.

Smell

Smell and taste are often referred to as the "chemical senses," for they respond to specific chemical molecules coming into contact with sensory receptors located in the nose and on the tongue.

One's sense of smell, or *olfaction*, originates in chemical receptors in the nasal cavity, which are connected to the brain by the first cranial nerve. This is rather fitting, because smell is the oldest and most primitive of the special senses. Many simpler creatures have more sophisticated senses of smell than do humans. Dogs, for instance, have a powerful sense of smell, and can readily identify other dogs (and humans) by sense of smell alone. The sense of smell in humans is of less day-to-day importance than vision and hearing, but is still important, particularly with respect to emotions and, some have argued, sexual behavior. (Certainly advertisements for perfume suggest this!) Smell is of special importance during the first days of life, when it is used by newborns of all species to identify their mothers.

The primary olfactory neurons that provide the basis of smell lie on the surfaces of the mucous membranes in the nasal cavity, and have surface receptors to distinguish different chemical molecules. It is estimated that these olfactory receptors can differentiate about 3,000 different odors.

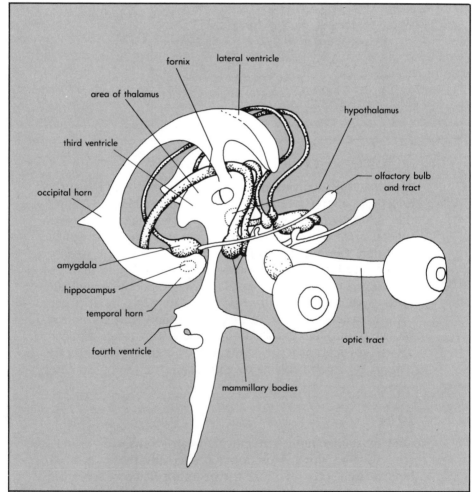

Figure 13: The Olfactory Bulb. Nerve fibers carry sensations of smell from the olfactory bulb, a long outgrowth of the brain, to the limbic system, the hypothalamus, and the reticular formation.

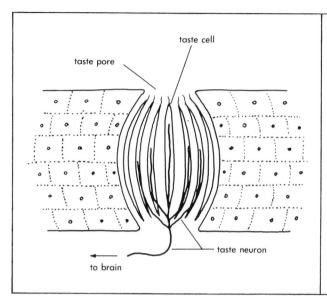

taste cell

taste pore

taste neuron

to brain

Figure 14: The Structure of a Taste Bud. *Each bud consists of about a dozen individual taste cells. Nerve fibers relay messages from the taste buds to a region in the sensory cortex.*

Olfactory Center in the Brain

The olfactory neurons are linked with neurons in the *olfactory bulb*, a long outgrowth of the brain. (See Fig. 13.) Fibers then carry sensations of smell from the olfactory bulb to several brain regions in the lower, more primitive part of the forebrain. Connections with the *limbic system* (see Chapter 6) account for the emotional aspects of smell, and may also explain why smells can quickly trigger certain memories. Links with the *hypothalamus* (see Chapter 6) can trigger visceral reactions — such as vomiting and nausea — in response to noxious odors. Other smells can cause vigorous arousal through olfactory connections with the reticular formation — which explains the stimulating action of "smelling salts."

Taste

One must first note that much of one's sense of "taste" is really due to smell. Most foods (especially those that have been heated) give off odors; the resulting olfactory sensations are often mistaken for taste. Thus, when one's nasal passage is blocked (for example, by the common cold), food loses much of its flavor.

Taste is mediated by taste buds on the tongue, which can perceive four primary taste sensations: sweet, sour, bitter, and salty. (See Fig. 14.) The taste buds responding to each of these different stimuli are arranged in special regions of the tongue.

Nerve fibers from the taste buds travel to the *gustatory* (taste) *center* in the brainstem. From there, taste sensations pass to a region near those of the mouth and tongue in the sensory cortex.

Although humans are neither the strongest nor the fastest of living creatures, they excel at coordinated, precise muscular activity.

CHAPTER 5

VOLUNTARY MOVEMENT

Life itself, as well as virtually all human interaction with the external world, depends upon muscular (or *motor*) activity. This is perhaps most evident in the rhythmic beating of one's heart: Synchronized contractions of muscles result in the vital flow of oxygenated blood throughout the body.

The cardiac muscles responsible for the heart's pumping action are largely controlled by the autonomic nervous system (see Chapter 1) and are not ordinarily subject to voluntary control. In contrast, the human body contains a powerful system of *skeletal muscles* which are used for voluntary movement. The shapes and sizes of these muscles vary. Large, strong *axial* muscles of the spine work to maintain one's erect posture. Groups of limb muscles centered in the shoulder and hip regions control the all-important movements of the arms and legs. Muscles in the head and neck are necessary for such basic human functions as eating and speech. Finally, the evolution of the complex arrangements of muscles in the wrist and hand has led to all the human accomplishments achieved by virtue of controlled, accurate movements of the fingers and thumb.

Muscular contractions are based on a complex arrangement of certain *proteins* in specialized muscle fibers. When properly stimulated, these proteins cause the fiber to contract. However, voluntary movement — whether of the limbs,

The human body contains a powerful system of skeletal muscles used for voluntary movement. Limb muscles, for example, control the movement of the arms and legs.

face, fingers, or any other outer body part — involves much more than mere muscular contraction. It must be planned and then carried out by using the proper set of muscles in coordination with sensory input and other sets of muscles. Although humans are neither the strongest nor fastest of living creatures, they excel at coordinated, precise muscular activity: the baseball pitcher throwing a strike at nearly 100 miles per hour (or the batter hitting a pitch for a home run); the ballet dancer moving gracefully through predetermined motions; the pianist playing a complex sonata. Perhaps most important, all forms of the *expression* of human thought depend on controlled voluntary muscular activity — from smiling and frowning to talking and writing.

This chapter describes the most important structures and systems, within and outside the central nervous system, that are involved in the planning, production, and coordination of voluntary movement.

Muscles

Muscles are made up of muscle fibers, of which there are three main types. (See Figure 15.) The *smooth-muscle fibers* are stimulated by the autonomic nervous system and are involved in involuntary movements of such internal organs as the stomach and intestines. Because smooth-muscle fibers are also organized in bands around blood vessels, sympathetic nerves supplying these muscle fibers can regulate blood pressure and divert blood flow from one region of the body to another by changing the diameter of specific blood vessels.

Cardiac-muscle fibers are specialized for heart function and form a branched network, within the individual muscle cells of the heart, that is interconnected at special junctions that allow electrical pulses to flow directly from the fibers

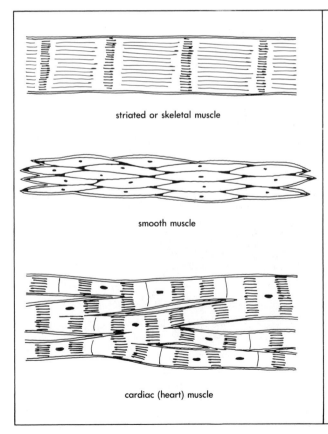

striated or skeletal muscle

smooth muscle

cardiac (heart) muscle

Figure 15: The Three Types of Muscle Fiber. *Whereas smooth muscle fibers, involved in involuntary movement, are relatively primitive, skeletal (striated) and cardiac muscle fibers are specialized for their more sophisticated functions.*

in one heart-muscle cell to the fibers in another. This in turn permits the masses of cardiac muscle that constitute the heart to contract in the organized, synchronized fashion necessary for the proper functioning of this vital organ as a pump.

Skeletal or *voluntary-muscle fibers* consist of highly organized arrangements of smaller fibers. These are also referred to as *striated-muscle* (meaning striped muscle) *fibers* because of the alternating dark and light bands of contractile proteins within them. A muscle such as the *biceps* in the arm is made up of many thousands of these striated muscle fibers, arranged more or less in parallel fashion. Such skeletal muscles are stimulated by *motor neurons*, the nerve cells whose cell bodies lie in the spinal cord or in the motor nuclei of the brainstem. The axons of these motor neurons leave the central nervous system through the spinal or cranial nerves (see Chapter 1), depending on their final destination.

It is important to note that more than one motor neuron stimulates a specific muscle. Each motor neuron acts on a group of muscle fibers — called a motor unit — within a spe-

The motor cortex is arranged by body region and varies from species to species. For example, apes use their toes more than humans do, so their toe motor area is much larger.

cific muscle. In general, the number of motor units in a muscle is related to the precision of movement that the muscle can achieve. Large postural muscles of the back and buttocks, involved only in fairly crude movements, are stimulated by relatively few motor neurons. In contrast, the precise movements of the fingers and eyes require smaller motor units with many motor neurons, each influencing smaller numbers of muscle fibers.

Most skeletal muscles are attached by tendons to specific locations on bones. Often they can be thought of as being arranged in pairs of opposing muscles. For example, the biceps muscle *flexes* (bends) the arm at the elbow joint, whereas the triceps, by means of a pulleylike action, *extends* or straightens the arm. This system of paired flexors and extensors, found in joints throughout the body, leads to much greater control of movement, because one muscle can serve to brake or otherwise regulate the contraction of another.

Control and coordination of voluntary movement are also made possible by specialized sensory receptors found in muscles and tendons. These position receptors inform the sensory and motor regions of the brain about joint position and the degree of tension of muscles. Analysis of such information is one of the key roles of the cerebellum, which we will discuss in further detail below.

The Motor Neuron

The ultimate neural control of muscular contractions is exercised by the motor neurons that activate the various motor units of the muscle in question. When stimulated, a motor neuron sends its electric pulse down to the *neuromuscular junction* — a synapselike region where the ends of nerve axons meet muscle fibers — in the motor unit it supplies and causes the muscle to contract.

There are a variety of influences upon these motor neurons. Some activate them and lead to muscular contraction, whereas others inhibit the motor neuron and prevent stimulation of its motor unit.

Motor neurons play a key role in bodily reflexes. For example, when a person steps on a tack, pain fibers from the foot enter the spinal cord (see Chapter 3) and send sensory signals to both the brain (so that the person is aware of the pain) and to motor neurons. These neurons in turn stimulate muscles in the knee to lift the foot off the sharp object.

Reflexes such as these are important, but are certainly not voluntary. Voluntary movement is the result of the co-ordinated stimulation and inhibition of motor neurons (and their respective muscles) by the important descending tracts arising from motor systems in the forebrain, brainstem, and cerebellum.

The Motor Cortex

The descending fibers most directly involved in the production of voluntary movement originate in neurons located in the *motor cortex*, which lies in each cerebral hemisphere just in front of the *sensory cortex*. The motor cortex is similar to the sensory cortex in two important ways. As with the "crossed" general sensory pathways, each hemisphere's motor cortex controls the muscles on the opposite side of the body. Thus, for example, if the functioning of the *right* motor cortex is impaired (most commonly by a *stroke*), muscles on the *left* side of the body will be weakened or paralyzed.

The motor cortex is also arranged by body region, as is the sensory cortex. Not surprisingly, some muscles require greater numbers of motor cortical neurons for their control than others. Thus the regions of the motor cortex dealing with the muscles of the face, hands, and tongue are larger than those involved with less frequently used, less complex, or less precise muscles such as those of the trunk, hips, and toes. (Of course, this varies from species to species. In apes, which use their toes to grip things in just the same way as they use their fingers, the "toe" motor area is accordingly enlarged.) The left side of Figure 16 is a map of the motor cortex, called the *motor homunculus*. (The right side of this figure is a graphic depiction of the sensory cortex.)

The motor cortex receives input from a variety of regions in the central nervous system — the sensory cortex, the premotor and supplementary motor areas (both of which will be discussed later on), the basal ganglia, and the cerebellum. Its major output is the *corticospinal tract*, which connects the motor cortex to the motor neurons in the spinal cord and brainstem. This descending tract also sends important branches to the other structures involved in motor activity.

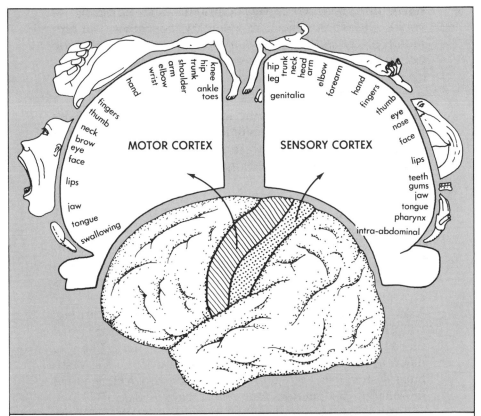

Figure 16: Cross Sections of the Motor Cortex and the Motor Homunculus and the Sensory Cortex and the Sensory Homunculus.
The homunculi (literally, "little men") are maps that depict the sizes of body parts in proportion to the amount of the cortex devoted to them.

Damage to the corticospinal tract can lead to a loss of voluntary movement below the level of the damage. Reflex activity in the affected muscles persists, however, and is even increased because of the loss of descending inhibitory fibers.

Movement Initiation and Coordination

As with many aspects of brain function, our understanding of how complex movement is initiated and coordinated is largely based on abnormal conditions in which such coordination does not occur. Research indicates that two regions of the brain — the *basal ganglia* of the forebrain and the *cerebellum*, attached to the brainstem — are critically involved with these aspects of voluntary movement. The *premotor cortex* and the *supplementary motor cortex* of the frontal lobe are also of great significance.

The Cerebellum

The cerebellum is one of the most fascinating parts of the human body, if only in terms of its structure. The cerebellum contains roughly half of all the neurons of the central nervous system, and the cerebellar cortex is one of the brain's most highly organized regions.

The cerebellum's importance in the regulation of voluntary movement is best illustrated by cases in which it has been damaged. Depending on the location of the injury within the cerebellum, the result can include loss of coordination of eye and limb movement, impaired balance, posture, and gait, and decreased muscle tone. Damage to this area may also disrupt the performance of acquired motor tasks, suggesting that the cerebellum plays a role in learning.

The cerebellum can be divided into three regions, each receiving a different neural input and sending nerve fibers to different targets. One region receives input from the vestibular system (via the eighth cranial nerve), as well as visual information. Its functions include the maintenance of balance and the coordination of eye movements with those of the head.

Another part of the cerebellum is concerned with the general execution of motor activity and acts by analyzing sensory input of all kinds and then influencing the activity of the motor cortex. This cerebellar region receives vestibular, visual, auditory, and general sensory information from all over the body. Proprioceptive — "position sense" — input into this region of the brain is especially important in coordinating the actions of muscles. Just as with the sensory and motor cortices, the musculature of the human body is "mapped" onto this region of the cerebellum. The portion dealing with the hands is especially large in humans.

The third part of the cerebellum is the most highly developed in humans. This does not receive general sensory input but receives fibers directly from the cerebral hemispheres — from the sensory, motor, and premotor cortices, as well as other cortical regions involved in movement. Through its output back to the premotor and motor areas it is thought to be involved in the planning and programming of movements. It may be especially important in rapid, pre-programmed movements, such as in swatting a fly or returning a tennis serve.

Some of the intoxicating effects of alcohol have to do with its disruption of the proper functioning of the cerebellum. Intoxication leads to problems of coordination and balance, slurred speech, and disturbed vision.

The Basal Ganglia

The basal ganglia are a collection of nuclei found in the lower portion of each hemisphere. Their importance is illustrated in one way by the vast amount of input they receive: Fibers pass from virtually every region of the cerebral cortex (and particularly from the motor cortex itself) to the basal ganglia. After processing within the basal ganglia, nerve signals pass back to the supplementary motor area and premotor cortex of the frontal lobe.

Much of what is known about the basal ganglia and their influence on motor activity stems from research into Parkinson's disease and other disorders of this region. "Parkinsonism" is characterized by tremor and other involuntary muscular activity, rigidity of muscles, postural problems such as stooping, and abnormal slowness of movement. Persons who have Parkinson's disease, which tends to afflict older people, also have difficulty initiating voluntary movement. It therefore seems that the basal ganglia normally act in the initiation of controlled, smooth voluntary movements.

It is now known that parkinsonism results from destruction of neurons in the *substantia nigra* of the basal ganglia. These neurons normally release the neurotransmitter dopamine at their synapses, and the drug *levadopa*, which is transformed into dopamine in the brain, is used to treat Parkinson's disease.

The basal ganglia have proven to be the indirect targets of certain illicit "designer" drugs. These drugs (made in a laboratory) are synthetic analogs, or "imitations" of other, legitimate prescription drugs, with chemical structures closely resembling those of these "parent" drugs. One such de-

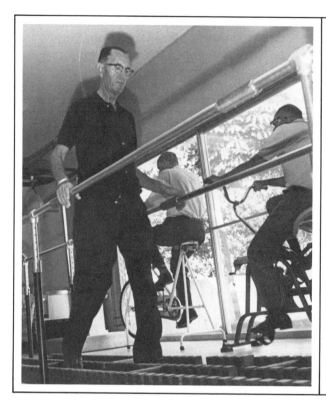

A patient undergoes physical therapy for Parkinson's disease, a disorder caused by destruction of neurons that release the neurotransmitter dopamine.

signer drug was supposed to be a street version of meperidine, a legal, prescription narcotic drug best known under the brand name Demerol. Meperidine is an opiate drug related to other opiates such as morphine and heroin. Like all opiates, it relieves pain, but also causes euphoria and is addicting. Tragically, a few batches of the new designer-drug imitation of meperidine were contaminated and caused parkinsonism in the drug's users, as well as in a chemist who was producing the designer drug, by destroying cells in the basal ganglia.

The Premotor Cortex and Supplementary Motor Area

The *premotor cortex* and *supplementary motor area* are both located in the frontal lobe of the brain and are closely associated with the motor cortex. Less is known about these areas than about others involved in voluntary movement, although there are some indications of their functions. The premotor cortex sends output fibers primarily to the reticular formation of the brainstem and specifically to those reticular neurons that influence the important muscles of the back, shoulders, hips, and thighs. It thus seems involved in the regulation of posture and in stabilizing the trunk and limbs during, for instance, complex hand motions.

The supplementary motor area receives input fibers from the basal ganglia and sends output back to the basal ganglia, the reticular formation, and the motor cortex, among other areas. The supplementary motor area is thought to be crucially involved in planning and initiating movement, as suggested by experimental results indicating that its neurons are active during the conscious planning of movements. The neurons were found to be activated even if the movement was only conceptualized and not actually carried out. Damage to this region can lead to complete loss of voluntary movement and speech.

The structures that govern emotion lie deep in the brain. To be sure, other species are capable of strong attachments, but humans are unique in the intensity and range of the feelings they experience.

CHAPTER 6

THE LIMBIC SYSTEM AND HYPOTHALAMUS

Together with our unparalleled language skills, probably nothing distinguishes us from other intelligent mammals so much as the complexity of our emotions. To be sure, other animals lead emotional lives as well, but it is only in our species that such emotions as joy, sorrow, love, and hate seem to be so intensely experienced and so powerfully expressed.

These emotions, along with the overall sophistication of the human sensory and motor systems, lead to behavior in humans that has a complexity not found in any other species. Human behavior is perhaps most distinguished by its unpredictable nature, in contrast with many lower species, whose actions, after some degree of study, can be fairly accurately foretold.

The study of human emotions and behavior, and the brain regions underlying them, is difficult, and less is known about these topics than about motor pathways or the visual system, for example. It is known, however, that two areas, the *limbic system* and the *hypothalamus*, are intimately involved both with emotional feelings and with certain types of fairly instinctive, survival-related behavior such as eating, drinking, and sexual activity.

This chapter briefly describes the limbic system and hypothalamus and discusses some of the ways in which they are thought to influence human emotions and behavior. It also examines the *pituitary gland*, which is closely linked to the hypothalamus and which powerfully influences many bodily functions and organs through the release of *hormones*. Furthermore, because portions of the limbic system appear to be involved in important memory processes, a short account of the neural basis of memory — so important in all aspects of life, and especially the emotions—is included.

Anatomical Overview

The various structures thought to be involved in producing emotions and instinctive behavior are buried deep in the brain and generally encircle the brainstem. The limbic system, which developed early in evolution (as did the hypothalamus), is made up of a number of discrete brain regions interconnected by nerve fibers. (See Figure 17.) That the part of the brain related to emotions and instincts is fundamentally old and similar in all mammals should come as no surprise: Feelings of fear, aggression, hunger, and sexual desire are, after all, basic to survival.

In other mammals especially, and to some degree in humans, there is a large olfactory input to the limbic system. This, too, makes intuitive sense, for many animals depend upon their sense of smell to determine what is good food, what (or who) should be avoided, and with whom they might mate. (When "in heat," females of most species release chemicals that have special odors to attract sexual partners.)

The structures of the limbic system operate like a central control box. They receive input from all the sensory systems, the association areas of the cerebral cortex involved in higher thought processes, and midbrain structures such as the reticular formation. Sensory input can affect emotions, for example, when we hear a song that has particular sentimental value to us, or see a hungry person on the street.

The output of the limbic system is similarly widespread, as one would imagine after considering the number of ways in which emotions express themselves: through visceral reactions (pupillary changes, tears, sweating, an increased heart rate, and other typical sympathetic effects), the release of

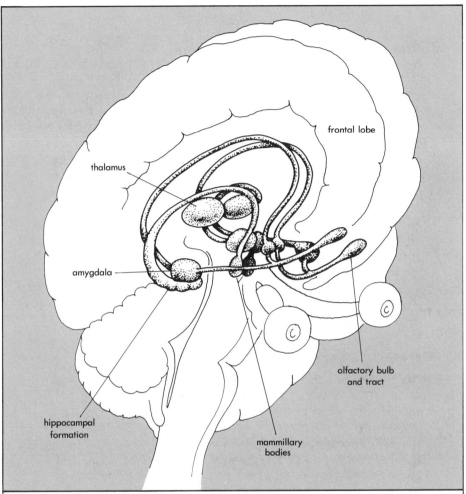

Figure 17: The Limbic System. *Wrapped around the top of the brain stem, the various structures of this system are critically involved in emotion and instinctive behavior.*

Inside the figure the following labels appear: frontal lobe, thalamus, amygdala, hippocampal formation, mammillary bodies, olfactory bulb and tract.

hormones, motor activity (facial expressions, for example), and language.

Much of the output of the limbic system goes to the hypothalamus, a tiny collection of nuclei located beneath the thalamus, in the midline of the central nervous system. This region is far more important than its small size suggests: Through its connections with the pituitary gland directly below it, it controls the body's hormonal system; it also contains critical nuclei that regulate the autonomic nervous system (see Chapter 1) and instinctive behavior.

The Pituitary Gland and Hormones

The pituitary gland is the body's master gland. It releases a variety of hormones into the bloodstream under the direction of the hypothalamus. Among the important hormones it releases are growth hormone (a deficiency or excess of which causes dwarfism or gigantism, respectively); sex hormones regulating sexual maturation, sperm formation, ovulation, and pregnancy; and hormones promoting milk production in nursing mothers. Hormones are similar to neurotransmitters in that they act on cellular receptors to cause certain effects. Unlike neurotransmitters, however, which travel only across tiny synaptic clefts between nerve cells, hormones are released from certain glands into the bloodstream and affect cells throughout the body.

Emotions and Drives

Complex human emotions are hard to describe accurately and equally hard to research. However, some brain regions have been associated with certain emotions, often by electrical *stimulation* or by surgical *destruction* of a particular region (the result of the latter is termed a *lesion*). The term *drive* (as in "sexual drive") is often used to describe instinctive behavior, which is typically related to survival. Currently, our understanding of human behavior is largely limited to understanding such drives.

Fear and Aggression

Fear and aggression are characterized by strong stimulation of the sympathetic nerves of the autonomic nervous system — popularly known as the "fight or flight" response. This seems to be coordinated to some degree by a cluster of neurons in the hypothalamus. Electrical stimulation of this region in cats provokes a dramatic display familiar to anyone who has seen a threatened cat: hissing, arching of the back, rising of the hair on end, and extending of the claws. Lesions created in the same area result in docility.

Cutting the neural connections between the cerebral cortex and the hypothalamus has caused cats to exhibit even more intensely aggressive behavior. This behavior, called "sham rage," is often spontaneous or provoked by subtle stimuli, such as a mild touch, that might ordinarily be ignored. Along with the elements described above, cats exhibiting this behavior may urinate, defecate, and even bite themselves. This suggests that higher cortical brain regions normally repress such behavior and that inappropriate sham rage results when this moderating influence is lost.

Damage to specific limbic structures lying deep within the temporal lobe can cause a variety of dramatic symptoms. Humans and other primates suffering from such damage demonstrate profound emotional and behavioral changes, most notably docility, loss or "flattening" of emotions, and submissiveness to other animals. *Hyperphagia*, a strange eating disorder in which almost any object is treated as food, can also result. Highly unusual and intense sexual behavior can occur as well, with the patient attempting to mate with different species or even inanimate objects.

The tiger trainer responds to situations of high tension and danger with the "fight or flight response," in which his nervous system marshals all his resources for survival.

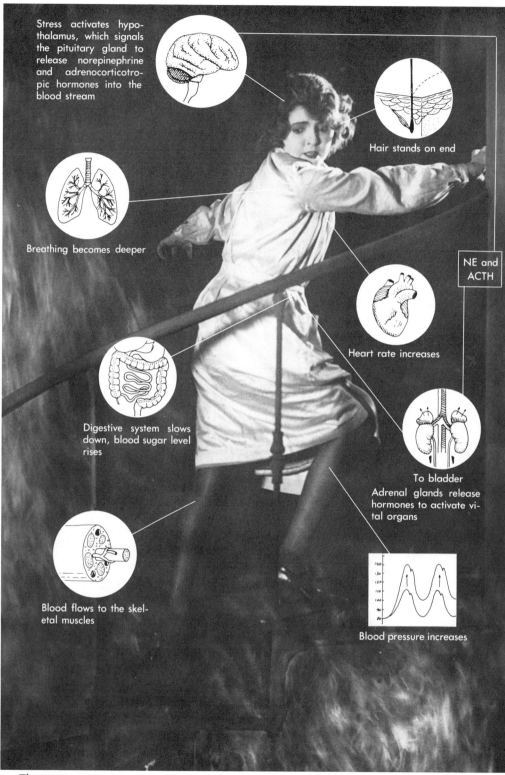

Stress activates hypothalamus, which signals the pituitary gland to release norepinephrine and adrenocorticotropic hormones into the blood stream

Hair stands on end

NE and ACTH

Breathing becomes deeper

Heart rate increases

Digestive system slows down, blood sugar level rises

To bladder
Adrenal glands release hormones to activate vital organs

Blood flows to the skeletal muscles

Blood pressure increases

The autonomic nervous system triggers a series of physiological reactions to moments of fear, menace, and peril.

Another case of temporal lobe dysfunction also illustrates on the one hand how certain aspects of human behavior seem to be controlled by specific limbic regions, and on the other how tenuous this control can be. In this case, a man with diseased temporal-lobe structures displayed a sudden, almost fanatic religious faith, obsessive writing habits, and hypersexuality.

Pleasure

With all this aggression bottled up inside one's brain, it may come as a relief to learn that there exist brain structures associated with pleasure. One so-called "pleasure center" is located in the hypothalamus, and as in the case of fear and aggression, has been demonstrated mainly through stimulation experiments using laboratory animals. For instance, rats with electrodes connected to this hypothalamic region in their brains would incessantly press a lever to stimulate the region and so experience pleasure. An area producing such pleasurable sensations when stimulated has also been located during neurosurgery in humans.

Because any "pleasure center" involves certain neurotransmitters, it is not surprising that various psychoactive drugs can cause pleasurable feelings by mimicking the actions of these natural substances. As mentioned in Chapter 2, cocaine and amphetamines stimulate the release of dopamine and norepinephrine, two natural neurotransmitters found in neurons of the limbic system. Opiate receptors — stimulated by morphine, heroin, and other narcotics — are also located throughout the limbic system. Presumably the euphoria caused by these drugs is linked to the stimulation of one or more such "pleasure centers."

Personality

Because the concept of "personality" is inherently more complex than that of a single emotion, it cannot be limited to a single cluster of nuclei or a single neurotransmitter within the brain. There is evidence, however, that the part of the cerebral cortex known as the *prefrontal cortex* within the frontal lobe is involved with personality traits such as planning and organization, ethical and moral sense, and overall control of emotions. ("Sham rage," referred to above, may result from the loss of such prefrontal control.)

The famous case of Phineas A. Gage and his "crowbar lobotomy" in 1848 is often cited in discussions of the prefrontal cortex and its relevance to personality. One day while he was working on a railroad, a sudden explosion sent a three-foot iron rod through Gage's skull, entering it in the jaw region and passing through and destroying his left frontal lobe. Amazingly, Gage survived (and even toured for a while with P. T. Barnum's circus as a sideshow "freak"), but his colleagues soon noticed profound changes in his personality. Before the accident, Gage had been well-liked, calm, and a steady worker; afterward he became exceedingly profane, tactless, disagreeable, and restless. It seems that some sort of civilizing or moderating influence on his behavior had been lost along with his frontal lobe.

The notorious "frontal lobotomy," frequently mentioned in films, represented an attempt by neurosurgeons to alter what were deemed dangerously aggressive or "deviant" personalities. This operation involved either the disruption of bundles of nerve fibers connecting frontal-lobe regions with other parts of the brain, or the creation of lesions within the frontal gray matter. Lobotomies have rarely been done since the 1950s, although recent advances in neurosurgical technology have led to reconsideration of such "psychosurgery."

The joke that "I'd rather have a bottle in front of me than a frontal lobotomy" is quite ironic, because the behavioral effects of alcohol seem in part to represent or at least resemble the loss of prefrontal control over normal behavior. Alcohol intoxication can lead to such "Gage-like" changes as increased vulgarity and profanity, loss of sexual restraint, and, most seriously, increased or unbridled aggression. It has been estimated that approximately one-half of all the violent crimes that occur each year in the United States are committed by persons under the influence of alcohol. Marital problems and domestic violence are also frequently provoked by alcohol.

Recent studies have provided the first evidence of links between a specific neurotransmitter and a particular personality trait. Psychiatric researchers measured the concentrations of dopamine in the brains of subjects and also quizzed these subjects about their personalities. The levels of dopamine were found to correlate with the degree of extroversion — a quality defined by such tendencies as talkativeness in small groups and "sensation-seeking behavior" — in the test subjects. Such preliminary experimental findings are, of course, far from conclusive, but they do suggest a possible mechanism whereby certain psychoactive drugs (such as cocaine, which increases dopamine activity) can affect a user's personality.

However, it must be emphasized again that one's personality is shaped by a variety of factors — some genetic and some environmental. Such variables as family size and income, position within the family (e.g., eldest, youngest, or only child), nutrition, body size and shape, and even chance can all affect personality development.

Hunger and Feeding

One's hunger drive, serving as an impetus to obtain and eat food, is clearly related to the survival of the individual and, by extension, the species. (There does seem to be a wide variation in the strength of this drive, accounting in part for individual tendencies toward being obese or thin.)

For many years hunger was thought to be controlled by two regions in the hypothalamus, known as the *feeding center* and the *satiety center*. Although this theory has now been discarded as too simplistic, the evidence on which it was based gives some indication of what sort of mechanism regulates an individual's eating behavior. In the research that led to the theory, lesions in the feeding centers of laboratory animals caused them to lose all interest in food, right to the point of starvation. Conversely, destruction of the satiety center resulted in animals with huge appetites that never seemed satisfied.

That one's hunger drive is influenced by other brain regions than the feeding and satiety centers has already been suggested by the symptoms of hyperphagia, the eating disorder discussed above that results from damage to limbic structures within the temporal lobe. In addition, special sugar receptors located in the hypothalamus monitor the blood levels of glucose (the primary sugar used by the body for energy) in the blood and stimulate eating when these levels are low. Amphetamines work as appetite suppressants, apparently by an action on hypothalamic neurons. (Tolerance to this effect develops rapidly, however, and the use of amphetamines to achieve weight loss is no longer medically recommended.)

Thirst

Control of the body's fluid volume is even more crucial than appetite control. The proper functioning of every cell in the body depends upon maintenance of a proper fluid environment consisting of water and ions, minerals, and proteins dissolved or suspended in this water.

The hypothalamus controls fluid intake in part by monitoring the amount of dissolved substances in the blood in order to determine how diluted the blood is, as well as the total volume of the blood. If too much water is present, urine flow increases and thirst is depressed. When a large water intake is necessary (such as after a large loss of blood or after general dehydration in hot weather), thirst increases to promote drinking, and the urine volume is decreased by the release of *antidiuretic hormone* (ADH) from the pituitary gland. Alcohol inhibits the release of this hormone, thus causing frequent urination.

Temperature Regulation

Temperature regulation is also of vital importance and is thought to be controlled by the hypothalamus. *Thermoreceptors* monitor body temperature and provoke actions designed to raise or lower the body temperature when necessary. When the body temperature falls, blood flow is diverted from the skin to deeper vessels (to prevent unnecessary cooling of the blood). When the body is too hot, sweating increases, as does blood flow to the skin, carrying and radiating heat away from the body. (Clearly, humans have also devised more sophisticated ways of controlling body temperature, including clothing, central heating, air conditioning, and hot-water bottles, to name but a few.)

Sexual Behavior

Although many books, films, and television programs may seem to suggest otherwise, the primary biological function of sexual activity is procreation rather than pleasure. Sex is clearly of the utmost importance to the survival of a species; this accounts for the strength of the sex drive. As noted previously, sexual arousal in most mammals is linked to chemical substances with distinctive odors that the female releases when she is in heat — the period when her ova (eggs) are ready to be fertilized. Called pheromones, these chemical substances stimulate males of the same species to attempt to mate with the female. (This phenomenon is well known to owners of female dogs or cats.) Males of many species also seek to attract females by a variety of techniques, ranging from displays of plumage to elaborate dances and songs.

Humans differ significantly from other mammalian species in that there is no period when a woman is "in heat" — although some women feel more sexually active after ovulation, when the egg is ready to receive sperm. Also in con-

The male of various species attempts to attract the opposite sex through a variety of wiles. Some employ exotic songs and dances; the male peacock proudly displays his colorful plumage.

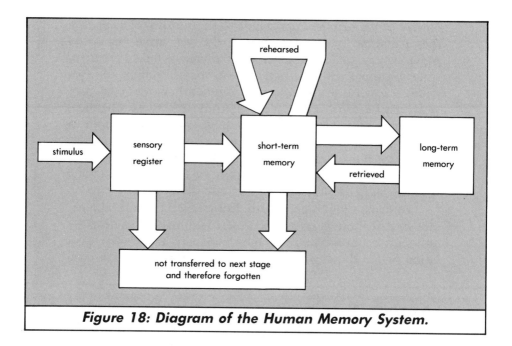

Figure 18: Diagram of the Human Memory System.

trast with other species, most human males seem relatively unconcerned by the presence or absence of pheromones, even though such chemicals may exist to stimulate the human male sex drive.

Sexual activity is moderated by one or more limbic regions located in the temporal lobe. Damage to these regions can result in hypersexuality, an abnormal condition demonstrated both by an increased sexual appetite and an indiscriminate choice of partners.

The powerful and uniquely human emotion of love is often linked to sexual arousal and activity. This sensation, romantically described as "infinitely mysterious" by one observer, might (rather unromantically) be considered to have evolved as a means of keeping couples together, thereby contributing to the procreation and raising of healthy offspring.

Memory

Memory remains a great mystery. Despite recent scientific progress, the basic mechanisms involved in the storage of thoughts, images, and emotions have not yet been identified.

Scientists refer to three basic types of memory. (See Fig.18.) *Sensory memory* is ultrashort — lasting less than a second — and is involved with the complete assimilation and initial processing of all sensory stimuli reaching the body. *Short-term memory* permits the transient memorization of an address or telephone number for a brief period. With constant rehearsal, however, selected items are stored in *long-term memory*, where they are later subject to retrieval.

More items are stored in long-term memory than are necessarily recalled. Cortical stimulation experiments have resulted in subjects' recollecting scenes they had long since "forgotten." Similar recall of long-lost memories has been produced by hypnosis.

Memory traces appear to be stored throughout the cerebral cortex; as we have already mentioned, one region in the temporal lobe, when stimulated, "releases" complex visual memories. The question of exactly how these traces are stored — sometimes for many decades — remains unresolved. One theory suggests that chemical changes take place in the proteins or nucleic acids of certain neurons, such as an increase in the production of a specific neurotransmitter. Other researchers suspect that the mechanism responsible for storing memories involves changes in the synaptic connections between nerve cells.

What is known for certain is that parts of the limbic system (notably the *hippocampus* and portions of the temporal lobe), are involved in memory *processing*. Several lines of evidence support this conclusion. One patient whose hippocampus had been surgically removed began to suffer from what is referred to as *anterograde amnesia*. In this condition, rather than past events being forgotten, nothing is put into long-term memory. The patient who experienced this could not remember the front page of a newspaper he had read two or three minutes previously, or someone he had met only half an hour beforehand. The dementia known as *Alzheimer's disease*, which can cause profound memory loss (see Chapter 8), is also known to involve widespread degeneration of hippocampal neurons. Long-term alcohol abuse can lead to *Korsakoff's syndrome*, which is characterized by a severe *retrograde amnesia* — the loss of past memories. Once again, it is part of the limbic system that is destroyed in this tragic disease.

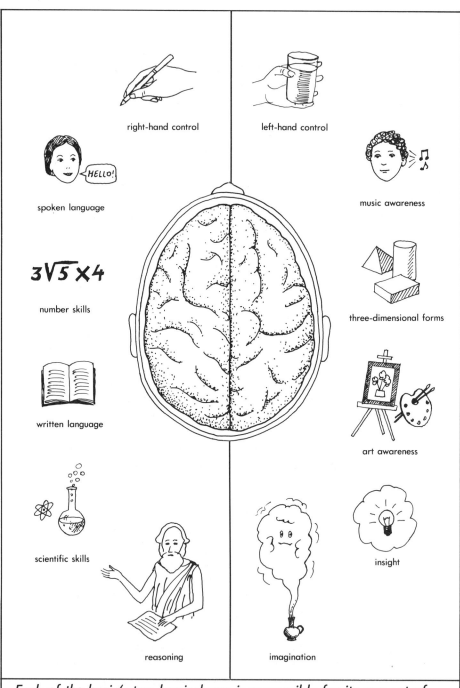

right-hand control

left-hand control

spoken language

music awareness

$3\sqrt{5} \times 4$

number skills

three-dimensional forms

written language

art awareness

scientific skills

insight

reasoning

imagination

Each of the brain's two hemispheres is responsible for its own set of functions. This diagram represents the different functions performed by the left brain and right brain in most people.

CHAPTER 7

LANGUAGE AND THE BRAIN

In its most fundamental sense, language represents the ability of one brain to communicate with other brains about its thoughts and feelings. By and large, this extraordinary talent (found in many species but most highly developed in humans) is taken for granted by all who use it. Each day we converse with friends, read newspapers or magazines, take notes in class or write a letter, and listen to the evening news or the latest song — all for the most part without any conscious effort. The importance of the development of a written language in particular tends not to be fully appreciated, integral though it is to civilization.

Soon after methodical research into language and the brain began in the 19th century, it became evident that, unlike the case with other, purely acquired skills, specific regions of the brain had evolved over time to permit what might be termed "intercranial communication." Evidence for this is found most dramatically in young children, who tend to become reasonably fluent in their native tongue by their fourth or fifth year — even without formal instruction. (Indeed, some prodigies can speak many languages at a very early age, suggesting that certain language centers in their brains are unusually highly developed.)

The search for these brain structures and the elucidation of how they function have been among the most fascinating and rewarding areas of neuroscientific research. This chapter discusses first some of the basic operations performed when one reads, writes, and converses. It then goes on to describe the organization of relevant brain regions, as well as some of the *aphasias*, or unique language disorders resulting from damage to these regions. Finally, the differences between the "right" and "left" brains, which have sparked much recent debate among neuroscientists, is also briefly considered.

Language Processes

Language consists of two different primary operations: *comprehension* and *production*. These tend to be performed at different times (reading a book or listening to the radio versus writing a letter or talking to a friend), but are sometimes done nearly simultaneously — such as while reading a prepared speech out loud. Not surprisingly, infants learn to comprehend many spoken words before actually producing speech themselves.

Comprehension of language involves mainly the auditory and visual systems, the first for spoken and the second for written language. Blind persons who "read" Braille with their highly sensitive fingertips depend on the sensory input from touch rather than sight, and the language systems of their brains adapt accordingly. Auditory comprehension is rather direct: Sounds transmitted to the brain by the auditory system are "translated" into recognizable words.

Reading, or comprehension of the written word, is a bit more complicated and involves a fascinating sequence of events. The eyes must first focus on the letters to be read; these are then recognized and processed as words. The rapidity and ease with which most literate adults can do this is best appreciated by comparing one's response to words written in native and foreign languages. For people whose native language is English, words in that language are understood immediately and without any effort. Words of a language such as French or German, which are written in the same alphabet, may make little if any sense, but are probably recognizable as names, nouns, and verbs. Words written in the Russian

Cyrillic alphabet are further removed from a native English speaker's comprehension. Finally, to the untrained eyes of the average Westerner, the "exotic" alphabets used in Japanese, Chinese, and Arab languages are completely incomprehensible, even in terms of knowing in which direction they run. The important point, of course, is that to native speakers (and readers) of those languages, these "strange" alphabets are read just as automatically as we read ours, and it is our alphabet that may appear to be made up of strange lines and squiggles.

Language production of all kinds involves the muscles of the body, that is, the motor system. In speech, the necessary sounds that make up a given desired word must be produced by the combined actions of the lungs, vocal cords, tongue, and lips. In writing, it is the intricate musculature of the hand that is most important for producing handwriting

Although learning to read is an enormously complex process, most of us learn to do so easily. The difficulty of deciphering a foreign alphabet highlights how much we accomplish in mastering our own.

(or even the more technological act of typing). In producing both written and oral language, the physical act of writing or speaking must be preceded by higher cortical activity that determines what is to be expressed.

Acts of combined language comprehension and production — the speechmaker reading from a text, or a stenographer taking dictation from his or her boss — involve a more complex system of neural pathways. The following section examines the regions of the brain involved in such sophisticated manipulation of language, as well as the more straightforward operations outlined above, and discusses how damage to these regions and pathways can lead to language disorders.

Language Centers in the Brain and the "Aphasias"

One of the first things about language and the brain to strike researchers was that much linguistic processing takes place in one brain hemisphere only — the so-called *dominant* hemisphere. Generally this is the left hemisphere, but in a few people the right hemisphere is dominant.

It is in one's dominant hemisphere that two crucial brain regions are found. (See Fig. 19.) *Broca's area* is located in the rear of the frontal lobe, close to the "face and tongue" portions of the motor cortex. Nearby, in the temporal lobe, is *Wernicke's area*. These two regions are linked by an important bundle of nerve fibers, as well as being connected to the visual, auditory, and motor areas of the brain.

Comprehension of language occurs in Wernicke's area. Spoken language heard by the auditory system travels first to the auditory cortex, as described earlier. Nerve fibers then carry these "sounds" (transformed, as always, into electric pulses) to Wernicke's area, where they are consciously recognized as words. Similarly, visual information encoding the shapes of letters and combinations of letters passes from the eye through the visual cortex and visual association areas, to Wernicke's area to be interpreted as words. The disorder known as *Wernicke's aphasia* leads to an inability to comprehend written or spoken language, although the person with this condition may still produce language.

Broca's area is concerned with language production — as its location near the motor cortex might suggest. It is here

90

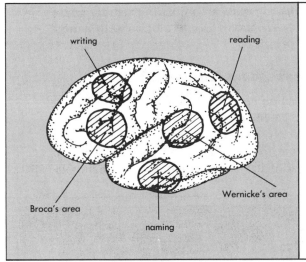

Figure 19: Broca's Area and Wernicke's Area. *These two regions of the brain are concerned with language production and language comprehension, respectively.*

writing

reading

Broca's area

naming

Wernicke's area

that words and phrases are formulated in terms of the neuromuscular actions necessary to express them. This region then signals the appropriate portions of the motor cortex (hand muscles for writing; facial and tongue muscles for speech) so as to produce language of the desired form. *Broca's aphasia* is thus a disorder of articulation: The patient understands written and spoken language perfectly well, but is unable to speak or write normally.

More complex operations are possible when the various language areas are used together. In the case of the public speaker reading a prepared text, the written words travel first to Wernicke's area via the visual cortex. The "decoded" impulses then travel from Wernicke's area to Broca's area, and then to the motor cortex for articulation. The language disorder known as *conduction aphasia* results when the link between language comprehension (in Wernicke's area) and language production (in Broca's area) is disrupted. Patients afflicted with this disorder will have trouble reading aloud or repeating phrases they have just heard.

In addition to the three primary aphasias just described, more specific ones have been noted in some patients. In a condition known as *alexia*, reading becomes difficult or impossible. The expressive equivalent of alexia is *agraphia*, in which writing is no longer possible. Patients with *anomia* may understand the *function* of an object but cannot name it — a pen would be described as "something to write with," but not named as "a pen."

Language and Hemispheric Differences

After discovering that one cerebral hemisphere (usually the left) is dominant for language production and comprehension, scientists wondered for many years what role, if any, the *non*-dominant hemisphere plays. The answer seems to be that there are regions in the right hemisphere analogous

Students study a foreign language in an audio laboratory. Patients with the language disorder known as conduction aphasia have trouble reading aloud and repeating phrases they have just heard.

to the language centers of the left, and that these are involved with the emotional aspects of language and communication.

Thus, in the "right brain" there is a region in the same location as Broca's area in the left brain, but which is concerned with producing emotional language. The normal intonations, rhythms, and other emotional subtleties of human speech are coordinated in this region. The right-sided equivalent of Wernicke's area serves to interpret this important aspect of speech. Other, similar right-brain functions include analysis of facial expressions and responding to the emotional content of music. Damage to or disease of these regions can cause *aprosodias* — conditions in which speech can become flat and emotionless, or in which the emotional (and highly significant) qualities of speech and gestures are not fully appreciated.

As one might intuitively suspect, there is a correlation between handedness and hemispheric dominance, although it is not absolute. The dominant hemisphere in right-handed people is always the left one. Curiously, this is true for most left-handers as well, although a small proportion of them have dominant right hemispheres, and some display no dominance whatsoever. Certain language disorders such as *dyslexia* (a reading disorder that may also include writing problems) and stuttering are more common in left-handed people, and it has been suggested that problems in the development of cerebral dominance may be the cause of these conditions.

The right brain seems to be specialized for other functions as well as governing and interpreting the emotional content of language. It is critically involved in the appreciation and interpretation of spatial relationships and the visualization of complex three-dimensional shapes. Recognition of faces (a form of spatial analysis) also occurs to a large degree in the right hemisphere. (In his book *The Man Who Mistook His Wife for a Hat*, neurologist Oliver Sacks describes a patient with a diseased right hemisphere who lost virtually all ability to recognize people — as the title suggests.) Just as some people seem more proficient at remembering faces or finding their way around the streets of an unfamiliar town, it seems likely that right-brain skills (just as left-brain ones) are more highly developed in some persons than in others.

Dyslexia is a reading disorder that may also include writing problems. It is more common among left-handed people and is thought to be caused by inadequate development of cerebral dominance.

One's power of attention may be centered in the right hemisphere. Patients with right-hemisphere damage sometimes seem completely unaware of portions of the left side of their body. An extreme example of this sort of phenomenon is also described by Dr. Sacks, in the above-mentioned book in a chapter entitled "The Man Who Fell Out of Bed." This involved a patient who was found on the floor next to his hospital bed, swearing that he had found someone else's detached left leg in bed with him that night. It was, of course, his own leg; the patient had evidently suffered damage to his right hemisphere that affected his ability to recognize his own leg!

Interestingly, hemispheric asymmetries and left-sided dominance for language are not unique to humans. It is now well established that certain birds use their left brains to produce their songs. A recent study suggests that in at least some strains of mice the left brain is used to appreciate the squeaks of communication emitted by fellow mice. Perhaps these findings will help scientists discover new information about the fascinating, and to a certain extent still-mysterious, link between the human brain and human language production and comprehension.

Rita Hayworth with her daughter Yasmin Khan in 1977. Ten years later, Hayworth died of Alzheimer's disease, a disorder characterized by progressive deterioration of the brain.

CHAPTER 8

BRAIN DISORDERS AND DYSFUNCTION

In discussing normal brain function, previous chapters have made frequent mention of various conditions in which the brain does not work properly — sometimes with fatal results. These disorders and cases of brain "dysfunction" not only are of great medical importance, but also have assisted researchers in understanding how the healthy brain works and in identifying the specific regions involved in particular functions. It was by analyzing patients with aphasias, for example, that the various regions of the brain dealing with language production and comprehension were identified.

This chapter briefly describes several common types of brain dysfunction. These various disorders illustrate that normal brain function can be disrupted in many ways: *Stroke*, for example, results from problems with the brain's blood vessels. *Epileptic seizures* occur when neurons display abnormal electrical activity. Traumatic damage to the brain or drug overdoses can result in *coma*. The dementia known as *Alzheimer's disease* involves actual neuronal decay. *Schizophrenia*, once regarded simply as a form of pure madness, is now thought to be caused by abnormal levels of a certain neurotransmitter, or defects in the receptors for this neu-

The world of the mental patient is a bleak one. Fortunately, current neuroscientific research is leading to the development of psychoactive drugs that can correct some of the brain malfunctions that result in mental illness.

rotransmitter. Of course, it is hardly surprising that the normal functioning of something so complex as the brain can be disturbed by a variety of causes.

Not only are these causes of medical, neuroscientific, and even general interest, but there exist important links between them and certain psychoactive drugs. For instance, cigarettes, alcohol, and cocaine have all been established as *risk factors* (agents increasing the likelihood of a certain disease) for strokes, as described below.

Stroke

Stroke, which is the third leading cause of death in the United States and the most common cause of brain dysfunction, is actually the result of a cerebrovascular "accident" that occurs within the brain. There are two types of such "accidents." The first is blood clotting in the vessels of the brain. This reduces or even stops blood flow to the region supplied by the obstructed vessel. The second type of accident is *hem-*

orrhaging, or bleeding. This occurs in weak vessels of the brain, usually when blood pressure is too high and the thin walls of the blood vessels burst.

In both forms of stroke, the brain region normally supplied by the blocked or burst vessel receives less or no fresh blood, and the death of neurons and supporting cells is the result. The actual *symptoms* of a stroke, which range from mild sensory loss to rapid death, depend upon the size and location of the regions affected by the decreased or absent blood flow and cell death. Frequently, a stroke affects the middle portion of a hemisphere, and therefore the motor and sensory cortices. Many stroke patients thus show loss of sensation and paralysis of muscles on the *other side* of the body. (Remember that motor and sensory tracts are "crossed" from one side of the brain to the opposite side of the body.) If the language centers of the dominant hemisphere are affected,

Stroke is the most common cause of brain dysfunction. Cigarettes, alcohol, and cocaine all heighten the risk of stroke.

the aphasias mentioned in the previous chapter can result. Often the visual pathways are disrupted, with ensuing impairment of vision.

Hypertension is perhaps the most important risk factor for strokes, but several common drugs are hazardous as well. The nicotine in cigarettes, for example, which increases the blood's viscosity and its tendency to clot, is clearly hazardous. (Women who smoke and use contraceptive pills are especially at risk for a stroke.) Heavy alcohol consumption leads to an increased blood pressure, and can also affect normal heart rhythm and function and increase the blood's viscosity — all factors that heighten the chances of a stroke. The recent rise in cocaine use (and especially of the powerful form of cocaine known as "crack") has provided dramatic evidence of a link between this stimulant and strokes. Cocaine rapidly increases the heart rate and blood pressure and can thus lead to a stroke even in young users of the drug.

Epilepsy

Epilepsy is a chronic disorder of the central nervous system. Symptoms of this condition are recurring fits, or seizures, ranging in severity from temporary loss of consciousness to life-threatening convulsions. These seizures, which are the results of spontaneous electrical activity within the brain, can occur for no apparent reason or be triggered by certain events. Flashing lights, television sets, and even video games have been known to cause epileptic attacks in people. Some medical researchers have suggested that the drinking of large amounts of diet beverages containing the artificial sweetener aspartame (Nutrasweet) may increase the risk of seizures.

As with strokes, the location of the problem in epilepsy is the key to the symptoms produced. In one relatively mild form of this disease known as "absence" or *petit mal* seizures, the victim simply loses consciousness for a few minutes before "waking up." This form of epilepsy often occurs in children or young people. The greatest dangers are related to what the person is doing when the seizure takes place; an "absence" seizure is clearly hazardous when driving a car or crossing a street. For this reason, airline pilots and others in similar occupations are carefully screened for epilepsy before being hired.

An engraving depicts the travail of two women with epilepsy, a chronic disease of the central nervous system.

The more striking *grand mal* type of epilepsy affects the motor system. Muscles, especially those of the limbs, first go rigid and then undergo jerking movements. Foaming at the mouth and involuntary jaw movements may also occur. If the mouth is opening and closing, the tongue may be bitten; damage to the skull from uncontrolled head motions is also a serious risk.

Other types of epilepsy are less dramatic and can involve only certain brain regions and functions. For instance, spontaneous activity in sensory centers can lead to "olfactory" or "gustatory" epileptic fits, during which a person experiences a sudden and strong sensation of smelling an odor or tasting food. The common sensation of *déjà vu* — the strange and mysterious feeling of having been in a certain place or situation before — results from a momentary and harmless form of epilepsy.

Alzheimer's Disease

Alzheimer's disease, a form of *dementia*, is a *degenerative* brain disorder. This frightening, tragic, and debilitating condition, like stroke, affects many elderly persons and the friends and families who must care for and worry about them. It has been estimated that as many as one of every ten persons over age 65 may suffer from Alzheimer's disease.

As of this writing, much remains to be learned about Alzheimer's disease. What is known is that as progressive deterioration of the brain takes place, different degrees of dementia are noted. Initially, the person with Alzheimer's disease may display only confusion and forgetfulness — the sort of absentmindedness often considered typical of the elderly. The dementia usually gets worse, however, and dates, times, and names are forgotten increasingly often. In the final stages of the disease, victims have trouble dressing and bathing themselves, walking, and engaging in other such basic activities. Memory loss grows even more severe, and language skills may deteriorate to the point where only strange cries and shrieks are produced.

Fortunately, a great deal of research is being done on the causes, diagnosis, and treatment of Alzheimer's disease, and although a cure remains a distant prospect, much progress has been made. One promising line of research involves the investigation of the disruption of normal *acetylcholine* circuits within the brain by the disease. Degeneration of hippocampal neurons, which normally release this neurotransmitter at synapses, seems to be related to the amnesia exhibited by Alzheimer's disease patients. Although these neurons can never grow back, some scientists believe that giving drugs containing acetylcholinelike agents can to some extent control the tragic memory loss.

Schizophrenia

The serious disorder known as schizophrenia is sometimes confused with "Dr. Jekyll and Mr. Hyde"-like *split personalities*. Schizophrenia is actually characterized by delusions, bizarre behavior, disordered thought, and other profound changes in personality and mood. It is a very real "madness" affecting roughly one of every hundred people throughout the world.

Four paintings of cats by early 20th-century British artist Louis Wain. In middle age, Wain developed symptoms of schizophrenia. His increasingly delusional state is captured in this series.

The schizophrenic patient may exhibit a range of symptoms. Paranoid delusions — the feeling of being persecuted, followed, or watched over — are often expressed. Auditory hallucinations, often of a critical or threatening nature, may also occur. Thought processes can become highly disordered, and the speech of patients with schizophrenia is often full of strange associations and trains of thought. Bizarre behavior and withdrawal from society may also be seen.

Persons affected by schizophrenia (along with other victims of mood disorders) once filled nearly half of all hospital beds and were "treated" in large mental institutions. The development of drug therapy for psychiatric illnesses has changed that, and most of the symptoms of schizophrenia can be treated with a variety of antischizophrenic agents.

By studying these drugs and by using other research techniques, scientists have established a link between schizophrenia and the neurotransmitter *dopamine*. As we have seen, in Parkinson's syndrome a *deficiency* of dopamine is involved, and patients are treated with drugs to increase the dopamine levels in their brain. In schizophrenia, however, therapeutic drugs work by limiting the actions of dopamine, by blocking its receptors on nerve cells. (An unfortunate side effect of some antischizophrenic drugs in some patients is the development of parkinsonian symptoms.) The most recent research indicates that persons with schizophrenia have an unusually large number of dopamine receptors in their brain. The long-term use of cocaine and amphetamines, which increase dopamine levels in the nervous system, leads to schizophreniclike changes in some users.

Coma

The term "coma" refers to a loss of consciousness. A coma, however, is not mere "sleep," from which one can be aroused; it is instead a very serious condition that often leads to death unless medical care is given promptly. A variety of common drugs, if taken in excess or in combination with other agents, can cause this dangerous condition.

The structures chiefly involved in coma are located within the brain stem. In particular, coma results from injury to or poisoning of the reticular formation (which as discussed earlier is involved in one's state of consciousness) and the "vital centers" regulating cardiac and respiratory activity. *Respiratory depression* is a special danger and a leading cause of death from coma.

All *central nervous system depressants* (for example, alcohol, barbiturates, and "minor" tranquilizers such as Valium and Librium) can lead to coma when taken in overdose, and they are especially dangerous when mixed together. Most drug-related hospital emergency admissions involve overdoses of these drugs, alone or "in combination" with other drugs, and a resulting coma. Opiate drugs (heroin, morphine, and codeine) can also lead to coma because of their powerful depressing effect on respiration.

Conclusion

It has been frequently asserted that the human brain is the most complicated object in the known universe. More passionate observers might describe it as the most incredible or most miraculous object. With its 10 billion nerve cells, linked together in a fantastically complex network of synaptic connections, the brain is at the center of all human survival, emotion, behavior, and activity. With this awareness of the power and uniqueness of each individual's brain, however, comes a sobering recognition of its ultimate fragility, and the ways in which its normal functioning can so tragically be disrupted by accident, disease, or drugs.

APPENDIX

State Agencies
for the Prevention and Treatment
of Drug Abuse

ALABAMA
Department of Mental Health
Division of Mental Illness and
  Substance Abuse Community
  Programs
200 Interstate Park Drive
P.O. Box 3710
Montgomery, AL 36193
(205) 271-9253

ALASKA
Department of Health and Social
  Services
Office of Alcoholism and Drug
  Abuse
Pouch H-05-F
Juneau, AK 99811
(907) 586-6201

ARIZONA
Department of Health Services
Division of Behavioral Health
  Services
Bureau of Community Services
Alcohol Abuse and Alcoholism
  Section
2500 East Van Buren
Phoenix, AZ 85008
(602) 255-1238

Department of Health Services
Division of Behavioral Health
  Services
Bureau of Community Services
Drug Abuse Section
2500 East Van Buren
Phoenix, AZ 85008
(602) 255-1240

ARKANSAS
Department of Human Services
Office of Alcohol and Drug Abuse
  Prevention
1515 West 7th Avenue
Suite 310
Little Rock, AR 72202
(501) 371-2603

CALIFORNIA
Department of Alcohol and Drug
  Abuse
111 Capitol Mall
Sacramento, CA 95814
(916) 445-1940

COLORADO
Department of Health
Alcohol and Drug Abuse Division
4210 East 11th Avenue
Denver, CO 80220
(303) 320-6137

CONNECTICUT
Alcohol and Drug Abuse
  Commission
999 Asylum Avenue
3rd Floor
Hartford, CT 06105
(203) 566-4145

DELAWARE
Division of Mental Health
Bureau of Alcoholism and Drug
  Abuse
1901 North Dupont Highway
Newcastle, DE 19720
(302) 421-6101

DISTRICT OF COLUMBIA
Department of Human Services
Office of Health Planning and
 Development
601 Indiana Avenue, NW
Suite 500
Washington, D.C. 20004
(202) 724-5641

FLORIDA
Department of Health and
 Rehabilitative Services
Alcoholic Rehabilitation Program
1317 Winewood Boulevard
Room 187A
Tallahassee, FL 32301
(904) 488-0396

Department of Health and
 Rehabilitative Services
Drug Abuse Program
1317 Winewood Boulevard
Building 6, Room 155
Tallahassee, FL 32301
(904) 488-0900

GEORGIA
Department of Human Resources
Division of Mental Health and
 Mental Retardation
Alcohol and Drug Section
618 Ponce De Leon Avenue, NE
Atlanta, GA 30365-2101
(404) 894-4785

HAWAII
Department of Health
Mental Health Division
Alcohol and Drug Abuse Branch
1250 Punch Bowl Street
P.O. Box 3378
Honolulu, HI 96801
(808) 548-4280

IDAHO
Department of Health and Welfare
Bureau of Preventive Medicine
Substance Abuse Section
450 West State
Boise, ID 83720
(208) 334-4368

ILLINOIS
Department of Mental Health and
 Developmental Disabilities
Division of Alcoholism
160 North La Salle Street
Room 1500
Chicago, IL 60601
(312) 793-2907

Illinois Dangerous Drugs
 Commission
300 North State Street
Suite 1500
Chicago, IL 60610
(312) 822-9860

INDIANA
Department of Mental Health
Division of Addiction Services
429 North Pennsylvania Street
Indianapolis, IN 46204
(317) 232-7816

IOWA
Department of Substance Abuse
505 5th Avenue
Insurance Exchange Building
Suite 202
Des Moines, IA 50319
(515) 281-3641

KANSAS
Department of Social Rehabilitation
Alcohol and Drug Abuse Services
2700 West 6th Street
Biddle Building
Topeka, KS 66606
(913) 296-3925

KENTUCKY
Cabinet for Human Resources
Department of Health Services
Substance Abuse Branch
275 East Main Street
Frankfort, KY 40601
(502) 564-2880

LOUISIANA
Department of Health and Human
  Resources
Office of Mental Health and
  Substance Abuse
655 North 5th Street
P.O. Box 4049
Baton Rouge, LA 70821
(504) 342-2565

MAINE
Department of Human Services
Office of Alcoholism and Drug
  Abuse Prevention
Bureau of Rehabilitation
32 Winthrop Street
Augusta, ME 04330
(207) 289-2781

MARYLAND
Alcoholism Control Administration
201 West Preston Street
Fourth Floor
Baltimore, MD 21201
(301) 383-2977

State Health Department
Drug Abuse Administration
201 West Preston Street
Baltimore, MD 21201
(301) 383-3312

MASSACHUSETTS
Department of Public Health
Division of Alcoholism
755 Boylston Street
Sixth Floor
Boston, MA 02116
(617) 727-1960

Department of Public Health
Division of Drug Rehabilitation
600 Washington Street
Boston, MA 02114
(617) 727-8617

MICHIGAN
Department of Public Health
Office of Substance Abuse Services
3500 North Logan Street
P.O. Box 30035
Lansing, MI 48909
(517) 373-8603

MINNESOTA
Department of Public Welfare
Chemical Dependency Program
  Division
Centennial Building
658 Cedar Street
4th Floor
Saint Paul, MN 55155
(612) 296-4614

MISSISSIPPI
Department of Mental Health
Division of Alcohol and Drug Abuse
1102 Robert E. Lee Building
Jackson, MS 39201
(601) 359-1297

MISSOURI
Department of Mental Health
Division of Alcoholism and Drug
  Abuse
2002 Missouri Boulevard
P.O. Box 687
Jefferson City, MO 65102
(314) 751-4942

MONTANA
Department of Institutions
Alcohol and Drug Abuse Division
1539 11th Avenue
Helena, MT 59620
(406) 449-2827

NEBRASKA
Department of Public Institutions
Division of Alcoholism and Drug
Abuse
801 West Van Dorn Street
P.O. Box 94728
Lincoln, NB 68509
(402) 471-2851, Ext. 415

NEVADA
Department of Human Resources
Bureau of Alcohol and Drug Abuse
505 East King Street
Carson City, NV 89710
(702) 885-4790

NEW HAMPSHIRE
Department of Health and Welfare
Office of Alcohol and Drug Abuse
   Prevention
Hazen Drive
Health and Welfare Building
Concord, NH 03301
(603) 271-4627

NEW JERSEY
Department of Health
Division of Alcoholism
129 East Hanover Street CN 362
Trenton, NJ 08625
(609) 292-8949

Department of Health
Division of Narcotic and Drug
   Abuse Control
129 East Hanover Street CN 362
Trenton, NJ 08625
(609) 292-8949

NEW MEXICO
Health and Environment Department
Behavioral Services Division
Substance Abuse Bureau
725 Saint Michaels Drive
P.O. Box 968
Santa Fe, NM 87503
(505) 984-0020, Ext. 304

NEW YORK
Division of Alcoholism and Alcohol
   Abuse
194 Washington Avenue
Albany, NY 12210
(518) 474-5417

Division of Substance Abuse
   Services
Executive Park South
Box 8200
Albany, NY 12203
(518) 457-7629

NORTH CAROLINA
Department of Human Resources
Division of Mental Health, Mental
   Retardation and Substance Abuse
   Services
Alcohol and Drug Abuse Services
325 North Salisbury Street
Albemarle Building
Raleigh, NC 27611
(919) 733-4670

NORTH DAKOTA
Department of Human Services
Division of Alcoholism and Drug
   Abuse
State Capitol Building
Bismarck, ND 58505
(701) 224-2767

OHIO
Department of Health
Division of Alcoholism
246 North High Street
P.O. Box 118
Columbus, OH 43216
(614) 466-3543

Department of Mental Health
Bureau of Drug Abuse
65 South Front Street
Columbus, OH 43215
(614) 466-9023

OKLAHOMA
Department of Mental Health
Alcohol and Drug Programs
4545 North Lincoln Boulevard
Suite 100 East Terrace
P.O. Box 53277
Oklahoma City, OK 73152
(405) 521-0044

OREGON
Department of Human Resources
Mental Health Division
Office of Programs for Alcohol and
  Drug Problems
2575 Bittern Street, NE
Salem, OR 97310
(503) 378-2163

PENNSYLVANIA
Department of Health
Office of Drug and Alcohol
  Programs
Commonwealth and Forster Avenues
Health and Welfare Building
P.O. Box 90
Harrisburg, PA 17108
(717) 787-9857

RHODE ISLAND
Department of Mental Health,
  Mental Retardation and Hospitals
Division of Substance Abuse
Substance Abuse Administration
  Building
Cranston, RI 02920
(401) 464-2091

SOUTH CAROLINA
Commission on Alcohol and Drug
  Abuse
3700 Forest Drive
Columbia, SC 29204
(803) 758-2521

SOUTH DAKOTA
Department of Health
Division of Alcohol and Drug Abuse
523 East Capitol, Joe Foss Building
Pierre, SD 57501
(605) 773-4806

TENNESSEE
Department of Mental Health and
  Mental Retardation
Alcohol and Drug Abuse Services
505 Deaderick Street
James K. Polk Building,
  Fourth Floor
Nashville, TN 37219
(615) 741-1921

TEXAS
Commission on Alcoholism
809 Sam Houston State Office
  Building
Austin, TX 78701
(512) 475-2577
Department of Community Affairs
Drug Abuse Prevention Division
2015 South Interstate Highway 35
P.O. Box 13166
Austin, TX 78711
(512) 443-4100

UTAH
Department of Social Services
Division of Alcoholism and Drugs
150 West North Temple
Suite 350
P.O. Box 2500
Salt Lake City, UT 84110
(801) 533-6532

VERMONT
Agency of Human Services
Department of Social and
  Rehabilitation Services
Alcohol and Drug Abuse Division
103 South Main Street
Waterbury, VT 05676
(802) 241-2170

VIRGINIA

Department of Mental Health and
  Mental Retardation
Division of Substance Abuse
109 Governor Street
P.O. Box 1797
Richmond, VA 23214
(804) 786-5313

WASHINGTON

Department of Social and Health
  Service
Bureau of Alcohol and Substance
  Abuse
Office Building—44 W
Olympia, WA 98504
(206) 753-5866

WEST VIRGINIA

Department of Health
Office of Behavioral Health Services
Division on Alcoholism and Drug
  Abuse
1800 Washington Street East
Building 3 Room 451
Charleston, WV 25305
(304) 348-2276

WISCONSIN

Department of Health and Social
  Services
Division of Community Services
Bureau of Community Programs
Alcohol and Other Drug Abuse
  Program Office
1 West Wilson Street
P.O. Box 7851
Madison, WI 53707
(608) 266-2717

WYOMING

Alcohol and Drug Abuse Programs
Hathaway Building
Cheyenne, WY 82002
(307) 777-7115, Ext. 7118

GUAM

Mental Health & Substance Abuse
  Agency
P.O. Box 20999
Guam 96921

PUERTO RICO

Department of Addiction Control
  Services
Alcohol Abuse Programs
P.O. Box B-Y Rio Piedras Station
Rio Piedras, PR 00928
(809) 763-5014

Department of Addiction Control
  Services
Drug Abuse Programs
P.O. Box B-Y Rio Piedras Station
Rio Piedras, PR 00928
(809) 764-8140

VIRGIN ISLANDS

Division of Mental Health,
  Alcoholism & Drug Dependency
  Services
P.O. Box 7329
Saint Thomas, Virgin Islands 00801
(809) 774-7265

AMERICAN SAMOA

LBJ Tropical Medical Center
Department of Mental Health Clinic
Pago Pago, American Samoa 96799

TRUST TERRITORIES

Director of Health Services
Office of the High Commissioner
Saipan, Trust Territories 96950

Further Reading

Angevine, Jay B., and Carl W. Cotman. *Principles of Neuroanatomy*. New York: Oxford University Press, 1981.

Bannister, Roger. *Brain's Clinical Neurology*. 5th ed. London: Oxford University Press, 1983.

Beardsley, Tim. "Sour Welcome for Aspartame." *Nature* 305, no. 175 (1983).

Cooper, J.R., F.E. Bloom, and R.H. Roth. *The Biochemical Basis of Neuropharmacology*. 5th ed. New York: Oxford University Press, 1986.

The Diagram Group. *The Brain: A User's Manual*. New York: Putnam, 1982.

Ellis, Harold. *Clinical Anatomy*. 7th ed. Oxford: Blackwell, 1983.

Fitzgerald, M.I.T. *Neuroanatomy Basic and Applied*. London: Balliere Tindall, 1985.

Gazzaniga, Michael S., Diana Sheen, and Bruce T. Volpe. *Functional Neuroscience*. New York: Harper & Row, 1979.

Goodman, Alfred, Louis S. Goodman, Theodore W. Rall, and Ferid Murad, eds. *Goodman and Gilman's The Pharmacological Basis of Therapeutics*. New York: Macmillan, 1985.

Hinds, Michael deCourcy. "They Fell in Love at First Sight." The *New York Times*, Feb. 14, 1981.

Haynes, Julian. *The Origin of Consciousness in the Breakdown of the Bicameral Mind*. Boston: Houghton Mifflin, 1977.

Kandel, Eric R., and James L. Schwartz. *Principles of Neural Science*. 2nd ed. New York: Elsevier, 1985.

King, Roy J., *et al.* "CSF Dopamine Levels Correlate with Extraversion in Depressed Patients." *Psychiatry Research* 19(1986): 305–310.

Marshall, John C. "First squeaks of speech?" *Nature* 325(1987):196.

Sacks, Oliver. *The Man Who Mistook His Wife for a Hat and Other Clinical Tales*. New York: Simon & Schuster, 1987.

Snyder, Solomon H. *Drugs and the Brain*. New York: Scientific American Library, 1986.

Thompson, Richard F. *The Brain*. New York: W. H. Freeman, 1985.

Wolf, Philip A. "Cigarettes, Alcohol, and Stroke." *New England Journal of Medicine* 315(1986): 1087–1088.

Wong, Dean F., Henry N. Wagner, Jr., Larry E. Tune, *et al.* "Positron Emission Tomography Reveals Elevated D2 Dopamine Receptors in Drug-Naive Schizophrenics." *Science* 234(1986):1558–1563.

Wurtman, Richard J. "Aspartame: Possible Effect on Seizure Susceptibility." *The Lancet*, Nov. 9, 1985, p.1060.

Glossary

acetylcholine chemical substance believed to be the major neurotransmitter

addiction a condition caused by repeated drug use, characterized by a compulsive urge to continue using the drug, a tendency to increase the dosage, and physiological and/or psychological dependence

analgesic any of a number of drugs used in the relief of pain

aphasia impairment or loss of the ability to use or comprehend words due to damage to language areas of the brain

autonomic nervous system the division of the nervous system that regulates such involuntary processes as breathing, digestion, and heart rate. It is subdivided into the sympathetic and parasympathetic divisions

axon the extended portion of the neuron that carries impulses away from the cell body to other cells and glands

basal ganglia four clusters of neurons at the base of the brain concerned with control of movement

brain stem the lower part of the brain, which connects the forebrain and midbrain to the spinal cord

Broca's area area on the left side of the brain that contains the motor speech area and controls movement of the tongue, lips, and vocal chords

cell body the part of the cell that contains its nucleus

central nervous system the brain and the spinal cord

central nervous system depressant a drug that depresses or lowers the activity of the brain and spinal cord

cerebellum the portion of the hindbrain that governs body movement and balance

cerebral cortex the area of the brain that governs higher functions, such as thought and language

cerebrovascular concerning the blood vessels of the brain

cerebrum the largest portion of the brain, consisting of the cerebral hemispheres and the basal ganglia

corpus striatum an area of the cerebrum that regulates motor behavior

dendrite one of many branched extensions of a neuron that receives information at synaptic junctions with other neurons and transmits it in electric form to the neuron's cell body and axon

dopamine a neurotransmitter that acts, among other places, in the corpus striatum. Dopamine deficiencies are implicated in Parkinson's disease

dyslexia a condition in which a person with normal vision is unable to interpret written language

endocrine glands organs that secrete hormones directly into the bloodstream. Included are the thyroid, pancreas, pituitary, and adrenal glands

endolymph a special fluid contained within the cochlea of the ear and the labyrinths of the vestibular system

gray matter regions of the central nervous system containing the cell bodies of neurons and other cells

hormone a chemical released into the blood from special glands. Hormones travel throughout the body to activate receptors located on specific organs

hypothalamus located at the base of the brain; involved in the regulation of thirst and hunger, sex drive, and body temperature. Also plays a vital role in governing the endocrine system and the emotions

limbic system a group of structures of the brain that are concerned with emotions and motivation

motor homunculus a map representing the body parts and their relative sizes according to how much of the motor cortex is devoted to each.

motor neuron a neuron that carries nerve impulses to muscles

neurotransmitter a chemical released by neurons that transmits nerve impulses across a synapse

oculomotor pertaining to the muscles that control the movements of the eye

olfaction the sense of smell

opiates compounds from the milky juices of the poppy plant including opium, morphine, codeine, and heroin

peripheral nervous system the entire nervous system outside the brain and spinal cord

physical dependence adaption of the body to the presence of a drug such that its absence produces withdrawal systems

psychological dependence a condition in which the drug user craves a drug to maintain a sense of well-being and feels discomfort when deprived of it

sedative hypnotic drugs drugs whose main effects are to produce relaxation, sedation, drowsiness, or sleep

sensory homunculus a map representing the body parts and their relative sizes according to how much of the sensory cortex is devoted to each.

substantia nigra a region of the basal ganglia, so called because it appears black to the naked eye. Problems within the substantia nigra cause Parkinson's disease

synapse the narrow gap between neurons, across which neurotransmitters pass to act on receptors

tolerance a decrease of susceptibility to the effects of a drug due to its continued administration, resulting in the user's need to increase the drug dosage in order to achieve the effects experienced previously

tract a bundle of nerve fibers concerned with the same function; typically passing through the spinal cord

vertebrae the important bones making up the backbone. The spinal cord passes through the vertebrae through holes in each bone

Wernicke's area the portion of the brain, located in the left temporal lobe, where language is processed and interpreted

white matter regions of the brain and spinal cord made up of groups of nerve fibers, or tracts

withdrawal the physiological and psychological effects of discontinued use of a drug

PICTURE CREDITS

Index

contraction, 61, 65
fibers, 61, 63–65
flexor and extensor pairs, 65
motor units, 64
reflexes, 65

nerves
cochlear, 54, 55
cranial, 29, 30, 38, 46, 54, 56, 64, 68
facial, 30
oculomotor, 30
olfactory, 30
optic, 30, 43, 49, 50, 51
parasympathetic, 31, 33, 34, 35
spinal, 29, 38, 46, 64, 65
sympathetic, 31, 33
trigeminal, 30
vagus, 30
nervous system *see* autonomic; central;
and peripheral nervous systems
neuroanatomy, 22
neuromuscular junction, 65
neurons, 25–28, 37, 38, 39, 46, 50, 51,
68, 69, 71, 82
electrical activity of, 28
features of, 26
mechanism of action, 26–27
motor, 37, 38, 64, 65–66
reticular formation, 39–40, 71
neurosciences, 22, 88
neurotransmitters, 21, 22, 26, 27, 28, 33,
40, 69, 76, 79, 102
chemical messengers, 22, 28
psychoactive drugs and, 28, 33, 79
stimulation of neurons, 26, 27–28
see also receptors
nicotine, 100
norepinephrine, 28, 40, 79

occipital lobe, 43
oculomotor nerve, 30
olfaction *see* smell
olfactory bulb, 58
olfactory nerve, 30
opiates, 28, 40, 46, 70, 79, 104
"natural," 46
see also heroin; morphine
optic nerve, 30, 43, 49, 50, 51
ossicles, 54
see also hearing

pain, 45, 46, 65
painkillers *see* analgesics
parietal lobe, 43, 46
Parkinson's disease, 41, 69, 102
peripheral nervous system (PNS), 25, 29
pheromones, 83, 84
photoreceptors, 50, 52
pituitary gland, 40, 74, 75, 76, 82
see also hypothalamus
prefrontal cortex, 66, 68, 70, 71
premotor cortex, 66, 68, 70, 71
pressure, 45
primary visual cortex, 51
proprioceptive information, 68
proteins, 61, 64
psychiatry, 22
psychoactive drugs, 27–28, 33, 35, 40, 79,
81, 98
psychology, 22
psychopharmacology, 22
psychosurgery, 80

receptors, 27, 28, 38, 39, 45, 46, 47, 50,
52, 56, 57, 65, 79, 81, 82, 102
cutaneous, 45, 46
density of, 47
dopamine, 104
hair cells, 54, 56
olfactory, 57
opiate, 46, 79
photoreceptors, 50, 52
position, 65
pressure, 39
sensory, 29, 45, 56, 65
sugar, 81
thermoreceptors, 82
visceral, 45, 46
see also neurotransmitters
reflex arcs, 45
reflexes, 39, 45, 65–66, 67
acoustic, 55
light, 52
vestibulo-ocular, 52, 56
visual turning, 52
respiratory depression, 104
respiratory system, 33, 39, 40
reticular formation (RF), 39–40, 55, 58,
71, 74, 104
effect of psychoactive drugs on, 40
function, 39

Paul Nordstrom August received a B.A. in English literature from Stanford University in 1980. In 1983 he moved to England in order to study medicine at Guy's Hospital Medical School in London. Special medical interests include public health policy, medical politics, and psychopharmacology.

Solomon H. Snyder, M.D. is Distinguished Service Professor of Neuroscience, Pharmacology and Psychiatry at The Johns Hopkins University School of Medicine. He has served as president of the Society for Neuroscience and in 1978 received the Albert Lasker Award in Medical Research. He has authored *Uses of Marijuana, Madness and the Brain, The Troubled Mind, Biological Aspects of Mental Disorder,* and edited *Perspective in Neuropharmacology: A Tribute to Julius Axelrod.* Professor Snyder was a research associate with Dr. Axelrod at the National Institutes of Health.

Barry L. Jacobs, Ph.D., is currently a professor in the program of neuroscience at Princeton University. Professor Jacobs is author of *Serotonin Neurotransmission and Behavior* and *Hallucinogens: Neurochemical, Behavioral and Clinical Perspectives.* He has written many journal articles in the field of neuroscience and contributed numerous chapters to books on behavior and brain science. He has been a member of several panels of the National Institute of Mental Health.

Joann Ellison Rodgers, M.S. (Columbia), became Deputy Director of Public Affairs and Director of Media Relations for the Johns Hopkins Medical Institutions in Baltimore, Maryland, in 1984 after 18 years as an award-winning science journalist and widely read columnist for the Hearst newspapers.

DATE DUE			